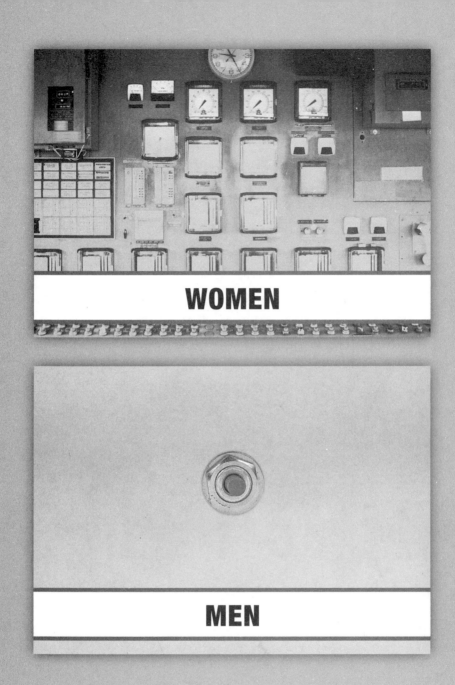

WOMEN

MEN

. . . GET IT?

WANT TO KNOW . . .

Who your guy really is when no one's looking?

What really makes him tick—and what ticks him off?

Why he sometimes treats you the way he does?

● ● ●

MEN AREN'T AS COMPLEX AS YOU THINK.
7 Things He'll Never Tell You opens the door to his inner world and reveals the simple things you can do to please and satisfy your guy and keep him around forever.

Why not take your relationship from ho-hum to exciting, from exasperating to fulfilling, from good to great? You can have the most satisfying partnership imaginable!

7 THINGS HE'LL NEVER TELL YOU

but you need to know

DR. KEVIN LEMAN

 TYNDALE HOUSE PUBLISHERS, INC., CAROL STREAM, ILLINOIS

Visit Tyndale's exciting Web site at www.tyndale.com

TYNDALE and Tyndale's quill logo are registered trademarks of Tyndale House Publishers, Inc.

7 Things He'll Never Tell You . . . But You Need to Know

Copyright © 2007 by Kevin Leman. All rights reserved.

Cover photo copyright © by Taxi / Getty Images. All rights reserved.

Interior photos © by Photos.com. All rights reserved.

Author photo copyright © 2006 by Tom Spitz Photography. All rights reserved.

Designed by Jessie McGrath

Edited by Ramona Cramer Tucker

Unless otherwise indicated, all Scripture quotations are taken from the Holy Bible, New International Version®. NIV®. Copyright © 1973, 1978, 1984 by International Bible Society. Used by permission of Zondervan. All rights reserved.

Scripture quotations marked TLB are taken from The Living Bible, copyright © 1971. Used by permission of Tyndale House Publishers, Inc., Carol Stream, Illinois 60188. All rights reserved.

To protect the privacy of those who have shared their stories with the author, some details and names have been changed.

Library of Congress Cataloging-in-Publication Data

Leman, Kevin.
 7 things he'll never tell you — but you need to know / Kevin Leman.
  p. cm.
 Includes bibliographical references.
 ISBN-13: 978-1-4143-1208-8 (hc)
 ISBN-10: 1-4143-1208-3 (hc)
 ISBN-13: 978-1-4143-1209-5 (sc)
 ISBN-10: 1-4143-1209-1 (sc)
 1. Men—Psychology. 2. Man-woman relationships. I. Title. II. Title: Seven things he'll never tell you—but you need to know.
 HQ1090.L455 2007
 155.3'32—dc22   2006037588

Printed in the United States of America

13 12 11 10 09 08 07
 7 6 5 4 3 2 1

*This book is affectionately dedicated
to my favorite daughter—that's what she calls herself—
Hannah Elizabeth Leman.*

*Mom and I are so very proud of the young
woman you have become.
I love you.*

Dad (and Mom, too)

● ● ●

CONTENTS

To my wonderful editor, Ramona Cramer Tucker.
I've come to expect excellence from you, and you always deliver it
in such a professional manner. You are appreciated.

INTRODUCTION

What a Man Really Craves ...

It only takes three things to satisfy your guy.
(Hint: They may not be what you think.)

● ● ●

I LIKE BEING A MAN.

It takes a woman an hour or two to get her nails done at the salon. But I can do my nails at a red light in 10 seconds or less with my front teeth. I even make it a game to see how many times I can hit my speedometer with my fingernails.

(If you're saying, "Eww, gross," you're definitely a woman. If you were a man, you'd be saying, "All right, score! I've got a whole pile on my dashboard.")

I could wear the same pair of Bermuda shorts day in, day out. It would never dawn on me to change them, unless I saw another pair waiting for me on my bedroom chair . . . or unless my wife, Sande, handed a new pair to me, told me to put them on, and whisked the old pair off to the washer.

I think I'm dressed up and ready for anything when my shirt has only one spot on it, and I'm in my standard T-shirt, shorts, tennis shoes, and baseball cap. It's how I dress 95 percent of the time.

The other day, as I was taking my wife a cup of coffee in bed, as I do every morning, my daughter Krissy showed up with my two grandkids, Conner and Adeline. I was so excited to see them that I sloshed a few drops of coffee on the kitchen floor. So what did I do? I took my sneaker and rubbed the drops around on the floor a bit, so they would dry faster.

"Daaad," Krissy said, rolling her eyes. "That is *so male.*"

And that's exactly what I am. A male.

I don't like to share my food with anybody. But I get first right of refusal on anything on Sande's plate.

I am as color-blind as anyone can get.

I never ask for directions.

I get antsy when you launch into a really long story. I can't help thinking, *What's the point?*

Sometimes I act like a four-year-old who has to have everything now . . . including *all* of your attention. Other times I am my wife's hero.

When I say things, I mean them. I like to say what needs to be said plainly. But when I'm quiet, I'm hoping you get the drift that I'm not crazy about what you're saying, but I don't want to hurt your feelings.

I'm a tough guy . . . but I'm tender underneath, especially where my family is concerned. (Just ask Krissy sometime how many times I cried when I found out she was engaged, when she tried on her wedding dress for the first time, when she walked down the aisle, when she told me she was pregnant with grandbabies one and two, and when I saw her holding those babies for the first time.)

Truth is, I'm no big puzzle. And neither is any man. We men and Simple Simon have a lot in common. The path to our heart is well marked, but it's also narrow, for there are few that we trust with it. Because for a guy, sharing your heart can be awfully risky.

FOR A GUY, SHARING YOUR HEART CAN BE
AWFULLY RISKY.

If you have picked up this book, good for you. You care about the men in your life, and you want to improve your relationships with them. Whether you are married, living together, dating, engaged, looking for that special someone, or you simply want to understand a son, brother, or father better, *7 Things He'd Never Tell You* will reveal the issues that are closest to a man's heart.

What makes a man tick.

What ticks him off.

And how you can have the most satisfying relationship with him possible.

When you date that special guy, you're always putting your best foot forward. Then you hook him, or he hooks you, and you decide you're both "keepers." You want to be in this relationship for a lifetime. You can't wait to never have to say good night and drive off to separate locations ever again. You envision romantic evenings together, wrapped in each other's arms, in front of the fireplace of your very own home.

Once the wedding is over, you concentrate on living life together. Settling into your careers, deciding who will do what around the house, who will keep track of the car's oil changes, pay the bills, etc. Somewhere in the midst of all this finagling is when you, a woman and a natural problem solver, get your first notion: *I don't remember that bugging me before. Did he always do that? How can I stop him from doing that?*

> What you put into your marriage is what you get out of your marriage.
>
> —Unknown

All of a sudden, there is a chasm between your expectations and the reality of living with your man. *Does he expect me to be his maid?* you wonder when you find the heap of dirty laundry under his side of the bed.

What's more important to him—hanging out with the guys or spending time with me? And if he likes "guy time," why does he act all hurt when I go out with a girlfriend?

I thought we talked about our budget. I've been sticking to it. And then he went and bought that plasma TV. We can't afford that. What was he thinking?

If he's an engineer, how come he never gets around to fixing our leaky faucet?

The list can grow. If you're not aware of the true needs of a man—what he dreams about, thinks about, and what motivates all he does—

disillusionment can set in. Misunderstanding can grow to anger and bitterness. You can begin thinking, *This sure isn't what I signed up for.*

Studies reveal that about 50 percent of those who marry today will end up divorced. And of the other 50 percent who stay together, only half of those are satisfied with their relationship.[1] No wonder the average marriage lasts only seven years.

So let me ask you: How satisfied are you *right now* with your relationship?

If you had a magic wand and could change one thing—little or big—about your man, what would it be?

QUIZ

How satisfied are you?

A. I could be with my man 24 hours a day and still want more. I never want to be away from him.

B. I love my guy, but it's nice to have a girlfriend break every once in a while.

C. The male testosterone fest in the garage is about to drive me crazy. Do I, a female, matter at all here?

D. Anybody here want to switch spouses for a day, a week, a year?

For answers, see page 177.

IF YOU COULD CHANGE ONE THING ABOUT YOUR MAN, WHAT WOULD IT BE?

HOME IMPROVEMENT, ANYONE?

Have you ever watched one of those home-improvement television shows? The ones that tell you how to beautify your home in a snap—and on a doable budget? The experts make it sound so easy. . . .

"From mess to showroom kitchen in 10 minutes or less."
"Eight quick ideas to make your family room more cozy."
"Take your bedroom from '70s brown to 2007 chic in a weekend."

But then what happens? You get all fired up to do the job . . . then find out it may be a little tougher than they made it sound. It may take a little longer than you thought. And it might be a little more expensive than you thought. But it certainly looks good when it's done. The time, expense, and any aggravation are worth it.

How about a different kind of home improvement? One that includes you and your guy? Most people in relationships live with an *expectancy* that they can change the other person. That if they just work hard enough, long enough, and if they nag enough, the other person will eventually change.

But that's a little like trying to rub the spots off a leopard. Sure, you can try to make that critter all one color by scraping his skin with a Brillo pad, but you won't wipe off those spots. You'll just irritate the leopard.

Makeovers work great with clothes, hair, and houses, but they don't work well with leopards or the men in your life.

Ever heard of the great reformer Martin Luther? His thinking and writings led to the Reformation, the transformation of much of church life and philosophy as we know it today. But his Brillo-pad personality also irritated a lot of folks along the way.

A woman who sets out to be a Martha Luther—a great reformer within her marriage—won't get very far before she irritates the man in her life enough to shut him down. So if you went into marriage thinking, *Well, I don't like that about him, but I can change that,* stop right there. Consider this truth: The boy or little girl you once were, you still are.

No one likes being told what to do . . . especially a man. If you want to catch a mouse, you have to put cheese—a mouse's favorite—in the trap. You can try pineapple, but all you'll be left with is an empty trap.

In the same way, you need to *understand* the male species before you try to change him. Otherwise you may have good intentions, but you'll be going about it the wrong way.

No matter how much society tries to make the two sexes androgynous, men and women clearly are different. Are they equal? Absolutely! But they are not the same.

When women talk about the man of their dreams, they use words such as *rugged, protective, handsome,* and *strong.* Yet the media is trying hard to turn the image of a man into a feminine, wimpy man-child. Someone who will be your girlfriend, who will go shopping with you, always see eye-to-eye, and give you the verbal and emotional strokes you long for.

But a happy marriage is one in which both partners understand, accept, and celebrate their differences. They enjoy relating to each other and seeing the world through each other's unique eyes. They cut each other some slack during pressured or tough times. (Before you get annoyed with your husband, just think of how annoying you are during that "special time" of the month. It'll put a lot of petty grievances into perspective.)

Couples who work together learn how to take stress not as a personal attack but as a challenge they can take on together. The key to growth and enrichment in marriage is in discovering ways to convey, "I understand how you feel and I'm going to do my best to meet your needs. I love you, and I'll be around forever."

Exactly what are a man's top needs?

THE THREE THINGS HE WANTS THE MOST

Recently when I was speaking at a Women of Faith event, I asked women this question: "What do you think is the number one need in a man's life?"

"Food!" a middle-aged woman called out.

Everyone laughed.

"The remote control!" a redhead chimed in.

More laughter from the audience.

"Sex!" a brunette added.

Groans from the audience.

"Okay, I expected that," I said, "but that's not true."

There was a dead pause, some confused-looking faces, and more than a few uplifted eyebrows.

"I'll get to that in a moment." I grinned. "What else do you think a man needs?"

"Basic things, like me taking time for him," an older woman added. "Admiration."

I nodded. "Yeah, that's really important. But what else?"

After some more answers, such as having a career, money, and success—none of which hit the target I was looking for—I could tell that the women were getting a little frustrated. I understood. After all, you women are the relational wonders of the world. You love to figure things out, and you're very good at it. You, of all people, ought to be able to figure out men.

Finally I said, "You don't need a PhD in analytical anything to decipher what makes him tick. Men are very simple to understand. But in order to do that, you need to know what's going on inside a man—at the core of the male psyche. It's only then that you'll be able to figure out ways to respond in a positive way to behaviors or words that may drive you crazy otherwise. But here's the deal: *You* are the ones who set everything in motion in your relationship. Because once you understand men, you realize that they are just little boys at heart. They want to please you and fear most of all hurting your feelings, because you might reject them."

Then I got down to brass tacks. I shared what a man's top three needs are—and said that these needs have everything to do with the woman in his life. You. These three needs have everything to do with the way your guy thinks, acts, and behaves. They are integral to the 7 things he'd never tell you . . . but you need to know. They are entirely accurate in 85 percent of marriages, for in 15 percent of marriages the couples' roles are switched. (If you are in that switched roles category, don't stop reading. You'll still find a lot of help in this book.)

So here they are: a man's top needs.

- to be respected
- to be needed
- to be fulfilled

What? Where's love in that mix? you might be asking. *Isn't love important to guys too?* Ask any guy if he'd rather be loved or respected and most would say respected. Because if a guy isn't respected, he doesn't feel loved.

IF A GUY ISN'T RESPECTED, HE DOESN'T FEEL LOVED.

Respect me.

Did you know how intimidating you women are? You're the schedule wonders of the world. What you manage to get done every day is paramount to climbing Mount Everest several times. Not only do you run our home smoothly, you make it look beautiful. You are an active part of school, neighborhood, community, and church events. You juggle my, your, and often our children's schedules effortlessly (at least it appears so to us). You remember birthdays, papers that have to be signed to go back to school, pets that need to be fed and walked, and doctors' appointments. Seventy-two percent of you also work outside the home—and get all that done too!

Frankly, sometimes what we men get done during the day doesn't seem to stack up to a whole lot when we hear the litany of what your day was like.

As the relational wonders of the world, women also seem to know everything that's going on in every arena you're involved in . . . as well as the latest gossip from the neighbors' houses. Because you have a need to talk and you love to talk, you get to know others quickly.

Here's what I mean: You get on a plane and sit next to another woman. Within the one-hour flight, you learn her name, what she's doing on that flight, the names and occupations of her two children, the best place to shop in Chicago for deals when you get off the plane, three stories about what her goofy husband has done lately, and much more.

Contrast that to this example: You get on a plane and sit next to a man. You try to engage him in conversation but it only extends to "Nice day, isn't it?"

The man bobs his head . . . once . . . and goes back to reading his newspaper. He has no need to go farther with a woman he has no relationship with.

If it's two men sitting next to each other, their entire conversation will be a simple nod over the newspaper. That's all that needs to be exchanged.

You see, a man has no need to talk. Because a woman, on average, uses three-and-a-half times as many words as a man every day, you are getting wound up to talk when your husband comes home from work. Contrast that to your guy, who has already used up his word count at work. Now he only wants to be silent. But that doesn't

> Marriage is like a three-speed gearbox: affection, friendship, love. It is not advisable to crash your gears and go right through to love straightaway. You need to ease your way through. The basis of love is respect, and that needs to be learned from affection and friendship.
>
> —Peter Ustinov

mean he's not willing to listen to you. He still wants to hear from you; he just may feel no need to contribute something immediately to the conversation. He wants you to respect him by filling him in on your day—especially on anything that is key to your family's life. (He really feels dissed if he hears about something thirdhand that has happened in his own family.)

You also show your respect by respecting him as an adult (even when he may act like a little boy). My wife, bless her, is a firstborn child. She's living proof about what I believe about firstborns. Firstborns *love* to tell people what to do.

For nearly 40 years, I've sat in my leather chair every morning, drinking a cup of coffee and watching FOX News. I also read the local rag and *USA Today* and then very unceremoniously drop them at the base of the chair. For nearly 40 years my dear Sandra has insisted on telling me to pick up the papers.

It's not that she wants to read the newspaper. She has no interest in the newspaper. But she loves to tell me—to remind me—and she's been doing it for nearly 40 years.

Do the math on that for a second: 365 days (unless it's a leap year) x 40 years = 14,600. That means she has reminded me 14,600 times to pick up the newspaper. Does she think that if she stopped telling me to pick up the newspaper it would somehow lie there, neglected and a mess, at the base of the chair? Does she really believe that I wouldn't remove it and take it to the garbage?

Take this case in point. Sande was going to be gone overnight on a Friday for a women's retreat. As she was walking out the door that evening, she asked me to go to Marie Callender's to pick up two lemon meringue pies the following morning since she wouldn't be home soon enough to bake any pies for our family event Saturday evening.

Saturday morning I got up and found a note:

> *Dear Leemie,*
> *I miss you already.*
> *Don't forget to pick up the pies.*

I smiled to myself. After all, I went to college for 13 years, so you think I could retain a thought from one night to the next morning. But that's Sande, God love her.

The same woman who nine days ago bought paint for the guy who is trying to restore our deck that was trashed by the floods. Where is that paint now? Still sitting on the brick steps next to the entry of our home where she left it when she removed it from her car. The rollers are there too.

Each day I walk by, see the paint and rollers again, and laugh. My newspaper has to be removed from the floor on the date that it's published. (In fact, right now it's 9:35 a.m., and I've already read through the paper and deposited it in the recycling bin. This is a norm in the Leman house.) Yet my dear wife's paint and rollers can sit there proudly, right by the entrance of our home, without bothering her.

Women, indeed, are a mystery.

But because I love Sande and understand those kinds of things about her, I sigh inwardly and let her tell me what to do . . . one more time. She certainly puts up with enough of my quirky personality for me to let the paper thing slide. And I get a chuckle each time I walk by her unfinished project.

The important thing is to give each other respect, even with the quirky things that could drive you crazy. Like dirty socks under the bed. Toothpaste on the sink. Phones that always travel from their base. Glasses that get left on the patio. As the old adage says, "Why major on the minors?"

We guys may look tough on the outside, but we're fragile on the inside. If we feel disrespected or put down, we'll get quiet and shut down. We'll begin to bury ourselves in work. We'll come home less and less. We'll seek other sources of respect—like working lots of overtime in the evenings and on the weekends, away from home.

WITHOUT RESPECT, THERE IS NOTHING TO BUILD YOUR RELATIONSHIP ON. NO FOUNDATION.

Without respect, there is nothing to build your relationship on. No foundation. Without respect, a man does not feel loved.

The number one need of a man is to feel respected . . . especially by you.

Need me.

Did you know that your guy is dependent on you? Because guys are less "relational," we tend to have a lot fewer friends. Sure, we have computer-game buddies, hunting, jogging, and at-the-gym-for-a-workout buddies, but they're more what you would call "acquaintances." Those of us who have one good buddy—my buddy Moonhead and I have been pals from way back—count ourselves fortunate. Consider this: In all the years we've known each other, Moonhead and I have only once talked for 36 minutes in a row. And that was when we were discussing a serious subject. But to have such a long-winded conversation is extremely rare for us . . . or any man.

Yet you, as a woman, don't consider it a real conversation unless it's at least three hours and 55 minutes long, and you've discussed multiple subjects from multiple angles!

Because men have fewer friends, you figure much higher in your guy's thoughts than you might think. In fact, the one person your husband cares most about is you. Although his ego may seem wrapped up in what he does professionally, don't let that fool you.

YOU FIGURE MUCH HIGHER IN YOUR GUY'S THOUGHTS THAN YOU MIGHT THINK.

Although men identify with their work—promotions, raises, backslaps for a job well done are immensely important to them— where your man really wants to succeed is at home. Underneath all his bravado, his grunts, his noncommunication at times, your man needs to be your hero. And what woman wouldn't want that for an end goal?

In fact, if you want a man who shows his love for you by surprising you with flowers, a man who is a great father, a man who always shows up for his kid's baseball games, a man who will be a warrior for you and your family, then here's the secret. He needs to be needed *by you.* He needs to hear that in your words and see that in your actions. He needs to hear you say to a girlfriend on the phone:

"Did you know what my wonderful husband did last week? The house was such a mess, and I really needed help. I was feeling overwhelmed since I have a project that's in crash status, and I've been working nonstop at the office. By Wednesday I was so tired I just wanted to cry. I didn't have the energy to even go grocery shopping before I headed home. I figured we'd be having soup out of a can for dinner.

"But guess what! When I walked in my front door, our living room was straightened up, the dirty breakfast dishes were in the dishwasher, and I could smell my favorite Chinese takeout. Oh, I love that man! He knew how much I needed his help."

He needs you to be efficient and independent . . . but not too efficient and independent. He needs you to allow him to do things for you, even if he doesn't do them quite the way you would do them.

HE NEEDS YOU TO BE EFFICIENT AND INDEPENDENT . . . BUT NOT TOO EFFICIENT AND INDEPENDENT.

You may be making a six-figure salary. You may be in charge of an entire day care. You may be running the lives of all four of your children—ages five through eighteen. You may feel like you're doing quite admirably on your own. At least most days.

But beware of being too independent, because then the message you're subtly giving the guy you love is *I don't really need you.* And what red-blooded guy wants to stick around when it's clear that he's not needed? That his contribution to the family—as a provider, a husband, a father—is not appreciated?

Men are a strange breed, I'll admit. If you treat us right and stroke us, we will purr like kittens and want to do everything to make you happy. And, unlike most cats who treat people like staff and not family, most of us will be loyal to the end of our days if you respect us and show that you need us.

If a man knows that his role in your family life can be played by no one else, he will be okay even when his company suddenly downsizes and he's out of a job. Even when his 20-something physique moves to 40-something flab. Even when he forgets your anniversary or makes a costly mistake with your finances.

The number two need of a man is to feel needed . . . especially by you.

Fulfill me.

When your guy picked you as his soul mate, he picked you for a reason. Here was his thinking: *I just met the woman of my dreams. I'm going to marry her, love her forever, and have her forever. She belongs to me. We'll have great sex forever.*

Then reality hit after the romance, the wedding, and the honeymoon. Life returned to "normal." He got busy with his job (or finding a job). You started to feel like Velcro woman—with everybody and everything sticking to you, wanting a piece of you. You became drained emotionally and physically, trying to meet everyone's needs all at once.

Because he had "gotten the marriage job done," he now turned his attention toward succeeding in his career and providing for his family. All of a sudden, you received fewer red roses, less romantic attention, and, let's be honest, sometimes started to feel as if you were his property but not his love.

> I chose my wife, as she did her wedding gown, for qualities that would wear well.
>
> —Oliver Goldsmith

Then, if and when kids entered the mix, your life as a family became even more complicated. You sometimes found your husband eagerly eyeing you and you knew exactly what he had on his mind. But you can't exactly put dinner on hold for a quick romp in the sack like you used to, since now you have a two-year-old screaming for food. Then there's the science project your fifth grader needs to finish by tomorrow.

By nine o'clock, when your kids are tucked in bed, you're exhausted. The last thing on your mind is satisfying anyone else's needs. After all, isn't that what you've done all day?

So once again, the man you married, who considered you "the woman of my dreams," is left with the leftover pieces of you. The I'm-too-pooped-to-whoop pieces.

And to your husband, sex is the third most important need.

Surprised? I doubt it. What you may not know is this: Sexual fulfillment is important to a man. But there's a difference between simply having sex and being sexually satisfied. Your attitude toward sex—whether assertive, aggressive, fun-loving or cold, noncaring, rote, let's-just-get-this-over-with—makes all the difference to your man.

Simply said, your husband needs sex—and he needs you to love it too. He longs to be intimate with the one person he trusts above all others, and that's you. If he feels fulfilled in his relationship with you, he will seek no others.

IF HE FEELS FULFILLED IN HIS RELATIONSHIP WITH YOU, HE WILL SEEK NO OTHERS.

Sex is an important ingredient in how fulfilled a man feels in life. But it is not the only ingredient. Your guy also needs to know that, in your world, he is the number one priority. That nobody else—including mother, father, girlfriends, or children—holds a candle to the importance he holds in your heart and life. He needs to hear you say on the phone to a girlfriend, "Oh, Anne, I've got to go. Jim just walked in the door." And he needs to not only hear your "Welcome home!" but feel your arms around him and your warm kiss . . . even if it is a quick one because your pot of water for macaroni and cheese is boiling over.

When you take time just for him (and not the leftover, bedraggled pieces of yourself that you have by late evening), a man feels treasured by you emotionally *and* physically.

The number three need of a man is to feel fulfilled . . . especially by you.

STRAIGHT TO THE HEART

When you look at your man, what do you see first? Do you see the kind of shoes or suit he's wearing? Do you critique whether he used the right belt as his accessory in his business-casual attire?

Or do you see your man's heart? What he tries to do for you and your family, even when sometimes he messes up? The expression on his face when he walks in the door—is he eager to tell you news, deflated because of something that happened, or feeling tired?

WE MEN ARE SIMPLE. IF OUR THREE BASIC NEEDS ARE FULFILLED, WE'LL BE BETTER HUSBANDS, BETTER DADS, AND BETTER LOVERS.

Is it easy for you to put your husband first? Or is it a struggle because of stresses in your relationship, a heavy workload, or too many commitments?

You don't have to be a rocket scientist to figure your man out. His three needs are basic—to be respected, needed, and fulfilled. If you understand these needs, and seek to fulfill them, you'll get a man who will protect you with the toughness of a pit bull but also one who will have the softness of a teddy bear toward you and your children (or any children you might have down the road).

You see, we men are simple. If our three basic needs are fulfilled, we'll be better husbands, better dads, and better lovers. And we'll be happily around for a lifetime. With just a little effort on your part, it's the best package deal around!

"MANSPEAK"

A MAN'S TOP THREE NEEDS

1. to be respected
2. to be needed
3. to be fulfilled

I JUST REVEALED A MAN'S THREE BASIC NEEDS.

These needs will affect everything about a man—how he feels about himself, his career, his home life, you, your relationship, and your future together.

But ask any man, "What do you wish the woman you love knew about you? What would you tell her if you could?" and he'll clam up.

Why is this? Because often the things that matter most to a man are also the ones he's afraid to verbalize. He's wary—often rightfully so—of how those statements will reflect on himself or how they'll affect the attitudes and responses of the woman he loves.

Yet deep within every man are the 7 things he'd never tell you...but you need to know. And each of these 7 things is intertwined inextricably with a man's three basic needs.

So on behalf of men everywhere, I'll be bold . . .

#1

THING HE'LL NEVER TELL YOU

"It's Thursday, and I'm out of words already."
("But if you want to keep talking,
honey, go ahead.")

Why men want the Cliff's Notes, and women want the whole novel.

● ● ●

IT WAS ONE of those evening social events I hate. The ones where you have to dress up, look your best, and try to act social even when it's not your thing and you're feeling strangled because your tie is too tight.

But because I love my wife, I agreed to accompany her...although, after we got there, I didn't see her for most of the evening.

I wandered around for a few minutes, giving others the nod and a smile, and finally ended up at the punch bowl. Somehow, when you're not feeling quite comfortable, it helps to be holding something.

After I had poured my punch as slowly as possible, I stepped back to scan the room and take the tiniest of sips.

Just then another man stepped up to the punch bowl. I gave him "the nod."

A nod is the universal man language, and it's easy to do. When you see another man, you raise your head half an inch. He raises his head half an inch back. You've just exchanged a whole conversation, and

1

you're both satisfied. You've both said, without saying it, "Hey, how are you doing? Great party, isn't it?"

But this guy at the punch bowl looked as lost as I felt.

Suddenly a streak of vulnerability came over me. I extended my hand. "I'm Kevin."

He shook it. "Rick."

"Great party, huh?" I added.

And then, right there, I'd run out of words. After all, this guy was a stranger. I didn't need to go farther with him.

Still we stood at the punch bowl.

So I tried again. "So . . . what do you do for a living?"

That little exchange filled another 30 seconds.

We'd run out of words again. What do you say when there's no recent ball game to talk about?

Then Sande walked by. A vision of loveliness in my eyes and, even better, my social rescuer. "Rick, this is my wife, Sande," I said, grasping my wife's arm.

The awkwardness was suddenly over. Sande stuck around and filled in the gaps for a few minutes with her lively personality, then whisked me away to introduce me to a couple other people.

I felt like a fish that had just been landed, flopping wildly and with bug eyes, on the deck of a boat. Then some kind soul said, "Oh, look at him" and had mercy on me and threw me back in the water, where I could breathe and be comfortable again.

Now let's say that you are a woman and you meet another woman named Carol for the first time at a party over a punch bowl.

"Hello," she says. "I'm Carol."

You introduce yourself and add, "Cute shoes."

"Oh, I got them at Macy's," she begins, and then the two of you are off and running. Even if you are a quiet woman by nature, within your 45-minute conversation, you'll talk about shoes, your dresses, where you love to shop, your favorite punch recipe, the places you visited this summer and what you loved about them, how you miss a friend who moved away, etc. And you know what? Although one of you is the vice president of a local bank and the other a nurse at a city hospital, what you do for a living doesn't even come up. You don't tend to talk shop.

But you both walk away with phone numbers written on napkins, waving good-bye and saying, "Hey, I'll call you." And what's more amazing to us men, you often do!

HEARING ≠ ANSWERING

Are we men just relational clods? Sometimes, yes. But consider that because women on average use three and a half times as many words as men (as I stated in the introduction to this book), when we get home from work, we're *done* with our word count. That means anything in the evening (when many social events occur) comes at us when we're feeling the *least* relational. Seriously, because we've had to exchange words all day to get the job done, a relationship with the remote control is looking awfully good. It doesn't ask us questions or get mad at us if we don't have a task done or if we don't answer a question a certain way.

That's why when you talk to us about anything, it's not that we don't want to *hear* you. It's often that we're not equipped to *answer* you at that very moment. But most of the time, even if we are in that easy chair, flipping channels with the remote control, we do hear you. It may just take us a while to process.

> WHEN YOU TALK TO US ABOUT ANYTHING, IT'S NOT THAT WE DON'T WANT TO HEAR YOU. IT'S OFTEN THAT WE'RE NOT EQUIPPED TO *ANSWER* YOU.

Remember that we're used to you running relational circles around us. Sometimes it takes us a while to catch up with you! But often what we hear mid-process is the "big sigh," then an irritated "Are you listening to me?" Frankly, it has taken twenty minutes to "detox" from work and figure out the next step on the project for tomorrow, and now we're starting to catch on to the fact that at the end of your long diatribe, there's a very important point. And it's something we definitely should know about . . . maybe even do something about.

Because women in general have a need to talk, to communicate, to process, sometimes a man will tune you out when the flow of words becomes too great. You know what I'm talking about—and exactly when that happens with your guy! His eyes start to glaze over, he focuses even more on the newspaper or the TV, and he starts to say "Uh-huh" to everything you say. What usually happens? You grow frantic to be understood, so you talk more, and the gap between you widens further.

Meanwhile, your guy is thinking, *Would you just stop talking and let the air recirculate in the room?*

It's no wonder this kind of scene happens, when you consider the differences between what men and women long for.

> The difficulty with marriage is that we fall in love with a personality, but must live with a character.
>
> —Peter DeVries

A WOMAN'S TOP THREE NEEDS

When I ask women what they want the most, I get responses like this:

"I want to be loved. I want to not only *know* I'm loved, I want him to tell me and show me that."

"I want to talk and know that he's hearing me. Sometimes I don't want an answer; I just want to process."

"I want him to be there for me and the kids. I want us to be his top priority."

"I want to be his soul mate."

"I want to hear about his day, and I want him to hear about mine . . . and care!"

"I want to know he is thinking about me during the day."

When I asked men at a recent marriage seminar what women want the most, one man blurted out loudly, "Visa!"

As his wife gave him the elbow, laughter broke out from the other men in the audience.

When you get right down to it, a woman's three basic needs are, in this order,

1. affection;
2. honest, open communication;
3. commitment to family.

Affection

More than anything, a woman needs affection. To a guy, affection means sex. To a woman, it means hugs, kisses, handholding, back rubs, a flower, or a sweet note for no reason. It means her man giving to her without having to have something back. She needs affection as *affection,* not simply as foreplay.

TO A GUY, AFFECTION MEANS SEX. TO A WOMAN, IT MEANS HUGS, KISSES, HANDHOLDING, BACK RUBS, A FLOWER, OR A SWEET NOTE FOR NO REASON.

I doubt there is a woman alive who would say, "I just love it when my husband grabs me!" A woman wants to be petted, caressed, embraced. And there is an unheard question that she asks of her man every day: "Do you really love me?" If her husband only shows her affection during sex, it won't be long before a woman will feel unloved. *After all,* she thinks, *he's only sweet to me when he wants sex.* And she's going to feel used—as if she's his property or an object, rather than the woman of her man's dreams . . . the woman he loves and cherishes more than anyone else on earth.

How does a woman feel cherished? When I asked a few women, here's what they said:

"When he tells me what a good mother I am."
"When he takes out the garbage without being asked on trash day."
"When he cleans up the mess I made in the kitchen."
"When he tells me I'm beautiful to him, even on the days I'm feeling fat and ugly."

A woman needs to know that she is loved for who she is, not simply for what she does. She needs to know her guy is thinking about her with affection and love at home and when he is away from home. As one woman told me, "Because I know he loves me, I can manage even the hardest of days and come out okay. His love gives my life purpose."

Honest, open communication

Did you know that scientific studies prove why a woman tends to be more "relational" than her male counterpart? A woman actually has more connecting fibers than a man does between the verbal and the emotional side of her brain. That means a woman's feelings and thoughts zip along quickly, like they're on an expressway, but a man's tend to poke slowly, as if he's walking and dragging his feet on a dirt road. Eventually his thoughts will catch up with the woman's, but it may be miles down the road.

In the miles in between is where women tend to get exasperated. After all, you're so good at expressing your feelings and jumping from topic to topic, who can blame you for rolling your eyes when all you get out of your guy is "the grunt"? To make matters more exasperating, he might call a buddy a minute after he's given you the grunt in response to your questions and launch into a 10-minute discussion about the size of the trout they caught last summer, what software program just went on sale, or that Cingular Wireless stock just went up.

Male-female communications expert Deborah Tannen, in her classic book, *You Just Don't Understand,* calls male-female communication "cross-cultural communication." She explains it this way:

> If women speak a language of connection and intimacy, while men speak and hear a language of status and independence, then communication between men and women can be cross-cultural communication, prey to a clash of conversational styles. Instead of different dialects, it has been said they speak different genderlects.[1]

Tannen goes on to say that when a husband and wife are sitting at a breakfast table and the man is reading a newspaper, there is a big difference in what women and men think talk is for:

> To him, talk is for information. So when his wife interrupts his reading, it must be to inform him of something that he needs to know. This being the case, she might as well tell him what she thinks he needs to know before he starts reading. But to her, talk is for interaction. Telling things is a way to show involvement, and listening is a way to show interest and caring. It is not an odd coincidence that she always thinks of things to tell him when he is reading. She feels the need for verbal interaction most keenly when he is (unaccountably, from her point of view) buried in the newspaper instead of talking to her.[2]

How do the different genders respond to this situation?

> To this man . . . a woman who objects to his reading the morning paper is trying to keep him from doing something essential and harmless. It's a violation of his independence—his freedom of action. But when a woman who expects her partner to talk to her is disappointed that he doesn't, she perceives his behavior as a failure of intimacy: He's keeping things from her; he's lost interest in her; he's pulling away.[3]

Are guys capable of talking? You bet. But the time to catch them is usually not the instant they walk in from work, when they're in front of the television, or when they're reading a magazine or newspaper. All three of those activities are saying, "I need my space."

If you want to converse with your man, pick your time wisely. You don't want to pick Sunday afternoon, during the fourth quarter of his beloved Bears game, to try to launch a conversation. One of the best ways is to watch something he's in the process of doing—such as building something out of wood in the garage—and say, "Wow, that looks interesting. Tell me more about that." Now you've got his attention. You've shown interest in one of his projects, and he'll be more than happy to talk with you.

If there's something you need or want to tell him, a great way to get his attention is simply to touch him. To your guy, your touch is powerful, and it can wonderfully open up communication lanes between you. As you're touching him, say, "Honey, I've got a really important question to ask you. You seem to be in deep thought, so now may not be the best time. If so, just let me know, and I'll wait until the time is right."

By touching him, you got his attention. By addressing him with respect, you secured his attention. And by giving him the choice of talking or not, you're almost guaranteed to have a captive listener!

Commitment to family

Children are pesty little buggers sometimes, and they can really get in the way of marital intimacy. But how much time your husband spends with your children and how he treats them has a lot to do with a woman's marital satisfaction. Generally, a woman feels comforted and loved by her husband when he goes out of his way to spend meaningful time with the kids. Why is this? Because those children and what happens in their days and their psyches are an extension of a woman's self.

Yet what often happens is that men are so busy pursuing their role of being breadwinner (we'll talk more about why this is so important to a guy later) that they are home less than you'd like them to be. They may even get home after the children are in bed . . . all because they are so committed to fulfilling their God-given drive to provide financially for their family.

Sadly, many men are not a significant part of their family's life. They may either feel like "that's not my job" or they may be unaware of why they feel so driven to succeed. They may even think subconsciously, *She does such a good job with them that she doesn't really need me.* Behind the scenes, he may feel like the little boy who doesn't have a place to go, so he's killing time by scuffing his shoe in the dirt, hoping to find some more pennies to bring home.

But nagging him will go nowhere. "If you *cared* about this family, you would have been at Jack's game!"

Instead, why not try this approach? "It means a lot to Jack that you took the time to be there today. Thanks for doing that!"

What guy wouldn't try to make it out of work early for the next game after hearing that?

For those of you who don't have children to think about in your relationship, think about how you feel when your husband goes over to your mother's house and helps her with a task she can't do on her own . . . without you bugging him about it. Doesn't that give you warm, fuzzy feelings for your man?

WE MEN ARE REALLY LITTLE BOYS AT HEART.
WE WANT TO PLEASE YOU.

When your guy goes out of his way for the family, tell him about it. Tell him how much you appreciate what he did. Remember that we men are really little boys at heart. We want to please you.

WHEN YOUR THREE BASIC NEEDS COLLIDE WITH HIS

Take a quick look at the needs of a man, and the needs of a woman, side by side:

A MAN'S TOP THREE NEEDS	A WOMAN'S TOP THREE NEEDS
1. to be respected	1. affection
2. to be needed	2. honest, open communication
3. to be fulfilled	3. commitment to family

Is it any wonder a woman's basic needs can conflict greatly with a man's basic needs to be respected, needed, and fulfilled? A woman wants to cuddle; a man craves sex. A woman wants to talk; a man has run out of words. A woman longs for the family to do everything together; a man longs for some independence.

THINGS YOU'LL NEVER HEAR FROM A MAN

- "Honey, can we just cuddle tonight and talk?"
- "If I took Friday off, could we go shopping and make a weekend of it?"
- "Is there any way we can get your mother to stay a week longer? She's only been here a month."
- "Of course, I'll go with you to the ballet. I love seeing those men in tights."

SHARING IS NOT THE KEY TO YOUR HUSBAND'S HEART, AS IT IS FOR YOURS.

One of the hardest things for a woman to realize is that sharing is not the key to your husband's heart, as it is for yours. You love words, sentences, complete thoughts, and paragraphs. You're in great command of your words, feelings, and thoughts. You are the Energizer Bunny of communicators who keeps going and going and going and going. . . . Your husband often feels like the bunny who has the wrong kind of batteries, lying mute on his side.

Here's the kicker: I wholeheartedly believe that your success or failure in marriage depends on how good you are at knowing your spouse's needs and meeting them.

And you, as a woman, can set all kinds of things in motion with the words you use with your husband. Your words can bring him joy and confidence, even when he feels like he's failed in some area, or they can shut him down. Then he'll be like Harry the tortoise, who hides under his enormously thick shell. He'll pull his arms and legs in. You could get the biggest pitchfork in the world and poke at him, to get him to move, but he'll refuse. He'll ignore you completely. In fact, he won't come out of that shell until you go away!

> YOUR SUCCESS OR FAILURE IN MARRIAGE DEPENDS ON HOW GOOD YOU ARE AT KNOWING YOUR SPOUSE'S NEEDS AND MEETING THEM.

WHY "WHY?" IS SUCH A CONVERSATION KILLER

All women love to ask questions. You're designed to ask questions.

But guess what? The best way to get into a man's mind and heart is *not* by asking questions. If you ask a man why, you shut him down because you put him on the defense.

"What do you mean?" you may ask. "I was simply asking nicely about his day, and he was starting to tell me what had happened over lunch. Because I wanted to know more about it, I asked him, 'John doesn't usually join you for lunch. Why did he join you today?' Then Kevin frowned, clammed up, and didn't say anything else. I just don't get it!"

Any guy who opens up to tell you something is already putting himself on the line to be ridiculed for a dumb move or for feeling the way he does. It's hard enough for a male to open his mouth to explain. Because you're such a natural information gatherer, and you want to know every detail, you ask why. But asking why makes your husband feel like *Oh, so you think I'm a loser because of the way I handled the situation? Do you think I'm stupid?*

Asking why is an immediate turnoff for a guy. Instead, the best thing you can do is to depress that "have to know" instinct. Simply listen, nod, show concern, and touch his arm in empathy or sympathy as he tells you what happened. If he's angry and he uses words you've never heard before, don't judge him. Don't say, "I can't believe you said that!" Don't judge his emotion. Instead, listen quietly as your

> The most important thing in communication is to hear what isn't being said.
>
> —Peter F. Drucker

husband struggles to put into words his thoughts and feelings about what happened. Don't jump immediately to say, "Well, I would have . . ." If you hear him completely out, you may be surprised to hear from his lips a depth of feeling you never knew was there: "I feel like such a failure. I'm not sure I can ever make it right. I don't know what got into me to say that to John. I'm worried I might lose my job over it."

When you are upset, do you always want answers? to be told what to do? Or do you sometimes only want to be heard? to process what happened by talking through it and having someone listen compassionately? Then give your guy the same benefit of your listening ear, minus the judgment.

Couples who listen without judgment are those who, step-by-step, can move their communication level from the typical clichés to sharing what matters the most. Those are the couples who will feel the ultimate fulfillment in marriage and will become each other's soul mates. Those are the couples who will stay together in the long haul.

Couples like Leon and his wife. I met Leon via the radio when I was in Medford, Oregon, to do a seminar on understanding marriage. My dear friend Perry Atkinson, the owner and general manager of the radio station KDOV there, asked me to call in to his radio station at 7:30 a.m. and give a little promotion for the seminar.

> The genius of communication is the ability to be both totally honest and totally kind at the same time.
>
> —John Powell,
> *The Secret of Staying in Love*

I was listening to KDOV, trying to figure out the right time to make the call, as Perry interviewed a guy named Leon about the weather. Just as I was about to dial the station, Perry said to Leon, "Kevin Leman is in town tonight, and he's going to talk about marriage. You've been married 59 years now, Leon. What's the one thing you'd suggest as most important to couples?"

"Mutual respect," Leon said.

Perry asked him something else, but it was obvious to me that Leon didn't catch everything that was said.

"Oh, and one more thing," Leon answered. "Just get one hearing aid."

One hearing aid? I thought. *What's that all about?* So I called in and said, "Hey, I want to talk to Leon. . . . Wait a minute! You say you've been married for 59 years—in a row?"

"You bet," Leon said and laughed.

"You said, 'Just get one hearing aid.' What did you mean by that in regard to marriage?" I asked.

"I've only got one hearing aid because I just don't want to hear it all," Leon replied simply.

Mutual respect and not hearing it all—wise advice for the longevity of a marriage. Especially with a verbal woman and her out-of-words-by-Thursday husband.

Leon and his wife have been married for 59 years, and they are still going strong. You and your husband can be one of those couples. And you can love your marriage along the way too!

QUIZ

How are you communicating?

There are many types of conversations you can exchange with your spouse.

- Clichés
- Facts
- Ideas/opinions
- Needs/feelings
- Complete personal truthfulness

Categorize each of the following statements with a C for Clichés, an F for Facts, an I for Ideas/Opinions, an N for Needs/Feelings, or a P for Personal Truthfulness.

___ "Good morning, honey!"

___ "Could you be home right after work on Wednesday? I need your help to get things thrown together before the Lewises come over for dinner."

___ "I miss Sadie. Could we get another dog?"

___ "I'll be home at five o'clock tonight."

___ "Francine just told me that Jordan joined the military. She and her husband were shocked."

___"Since I saw that TV program about breast cancer, it's been on my mind. I worry that I might get it sometime. Then what would happen to you? the kids?"

___ "Do you think we should set aside some money for a special vacation next year since it's our tenth anniversary?"

___ "And how was your day?"

___ "It's going to be cold today."

___ "I'm taking Angie shopping for a new coat. She's growing."

___ "Ever since mom died, I can't shake this lonely feeling I have. I feel like I've lost not only my mom, but part of myself."

For answers, see page 179.

Which of the types of conversations are most common in your relationship? Why?

"MANSPEAK"

TALK HIS LANGUAGE

If you feel compelled to tell your guy something, try these:

1. Tell him what a great husband he is.
2. Tell him what a great dad he is.
3. Tell him what a great job he does as a provider for your family.
4. Tell him what a great lover he is.

ON MOTHER'S DAY I ALWAYS TRY TO DO THINGS UP RIGHT. One year I really did things right. I made reservations at the nicest resort in town. The bill I received would choke a horse, but it was worth it. And as Sande said, she loved it because there was no Jell-O in sight.

As part of my tribute to my wife, I decided on the spur of the moment to say to our kids, "This would be a real appropriate time for you to share with your mom what you appreciate most about her."

"Food!" my secondborn said immediately.

That was it. She didn't say anything else. Just food.

Well, this isn't playing out very well, I thought. *So much for the sweet things I was hoping my kids would say on such an occasion.*

But when I thought about Krissy's response later, I realized that it was truthful and a great compliment. After all, Krissy was then a rapidly growing 15-year-old and an athlete, and she'd come home ravenous after school and practice. Sande is not just a good cook, but a great cook. So Krissy was simply showing her appreciation for one of her mother's skills that meant the most to her right then.

STRAIGHT FROM THE HEART

That's exactly what your guy needs to hear from you—your appreciation. But in order for him to hear it, you need to be able to speak his
language.

Let him detox.

Can people change
their conversational
styles? Yes, they
can—to an extent.
But those who
ask this question
rarely want to
change their own
styles. Usually,
what they have
in mind is sending
their partners for
repair.

—Deborah Tannen[4]

Why not give him a few minutes to "detox"—even a half
hour—when he first gets home from work? Then he'll be
happy to hear about your day and any concerns. When
he steps into the house, what he really wants to do is
take a leak. He needs time alone . . . to decompress.
Often the best place to do that is in the bathroom, where
he's less likely to be interrupted.

Dads, especially, need to decompress before they
arrive home. It's why I suggest to men that on stressful
days they choose their radio station or CD appropriately.
They need to find some elevator music to wind them
down.

One couple we know has changed their strategy
twice already in their 15-year marriage. When they were
childless and both held full-time jobs, they agreed to take
a "quiet half hour" after each got home before they began
to talk and make dinner together. But when children
came along, they agreed that when he'd had a particularly intense day, he would arrive home half an hour later
from work. In-between he'd go to a local park and would
take a half-hour walk to get any work questions out of his
brain so he could be "home centered" when he got home.

Their children are now three and five. It's important that the kids who
yell "Daddy!" and swarm him as soon as they see him do indeed get their
daddy's immediate time and attention.

Just the facts please, ma'am.

Realize that he is designed to want "just the facts, ma'am." He
doesn't need all the nuances, details, emotion, or who said what
when, and a repeat of the entire conversation that upset you. He
needs the facts:

- You're upset.
- You had a conversation today with X.
- The main point.
- What you want him to do about it (if anything).

If you are desperate to share every detail, talk to a girlfriend! But don't talk to that girlfriend first if it has anything to do with your guy, being upset with your guy, or something that happened in your family that he should know first.

Say what you mean; mean what you say.

We guys are simple folks. When we talk, we say what we mean. Perhaps that's one of the reasons why we get so befuddled by a woman's words.

Consider this recent conversation in our house. Keep in mind that Sande and I have been married for 38 years:

My wife and I and several of our kids were sitting around the dinner table. We were having pork and applesauce, one of my favorite meals. I'd been smelling it for the last hour and, I tell you, there are few aromas more heavenly to me.

Right after the blessing, I said to Sande, "Honey, pass me the applesauce, will you?"

She paused. "Oh. You don't want that applesauce."

I wrinkled a brow. "Why not?"

"Well," she said slowly, "there's too much sugar in it."

Mmm, I was thinking to myself. *If I don't want it, why did I ask for it? And if it doesn't taste good, why is it on the table? It's homemade applesauce too. Not that excuse for applesauce you find in the store.*

After all, we're the kind of house where all the cookies are made from scratch. (Store-bought are Satan's cookies, in my humble wife's opinion.)

What was my wife trying to say under the surface? I could figure out only two options:

1. Was she trying to tell me I'm too fat and don't need all that applesauce?
2. Since she's such a perfectionistic cook, did she mistakenly add too much sugar and feels bad about it not tasting "just right"? But then it wouldn't be like Sande to put a failed effort on the table.

You see what I mean, ladies? We men often find ourselves scratching our heads, trying to figure out what your words are really saying.

There's a tradition in the Leman house. It began when my children complained about me being so hard to buy for because I have such distinctive tastes. One year, tired of listening to the complaints, I decided that around Thanksgiving, I'd go to the malls and stores and buy myself Christmas gifts: sweaters, aftershave, a shirt, a belt, cologne, and any other stuff I could find that represented a wide variety of gifts and prices. On Thanksgiving, when my family gathered together, they could draw straws (the kids, that is) to see who got to go first in "Dad's store" once it was officially open. By Dad's store, I mean that the items are strewn very lovingly on the couch, chairs, etc., in our living room. The only rule is that you can buy one gift at a time. That makes it fair for everyone.

> Communication isn't just talking. It's talking in a way that the other person can receive it.
>
> —Unknown

Dad's store was such a hit that we've done it every year since. The kids were so relieved not to have to shop for me. But this last Thanksgiving, I was left holding the bag (literally) for one gift that didn't get bought. It was a V-neck, red cashmere sweater. I'd been so proud of that purchase because I got it for a real steal, so I figured somebody would snatch it up from Dad's store. But nobody in my family seemed interested in purchasing that sweater. So it hung around in the living room.

Just before Christmas, the local women's Bible study groups had their closing session. It's always a luncheon. This year, they asked me to be their speaker. So I said to my wife, "Uh, honey, come in here a moment." By "here" I meant the living room, where the red sweater was still draped over the sofa. "Do you like this sweater? Should I think about wearing it to the women's event?"

Sande shuffled her feet and didn't quite meet my eyes, "Well, you need a Christmas sweater."

Now I *know* there's not a man in the universe who *needs* a Christmas sweater. Most of us have way too many of those offerings stuffed at the back of our closets or under our beds because we're too afraid to take them back and offend somebody.

So I asked her, "Do you like the sweater?"

She still didn't meet my eyes. "You go ahead and wear it."

So now I've asked her twice. She's told me I need a Christmas sweater and that I could wear it to the function, neither of which is what I want to hear. What I want to know simply is, does she like it or doesn't she?

If she said to me, "I don't like it," I'd take it back and be 70 bucks richer. No big deal. I just want to know.

But Sande gave me what I call the typical woman's response. She didn't want to say bluntly, "Leemie, I do *not* like that sweater."

This is the same lovely bride who, when I have a rough day doing a TV show and get a lot of nasty letters from people who don't like anything I said from the time I said hello to the time I said good-bye, will read the letters I share with her. Then she'll look up and say bluntly, "Hey, Leemie, it's easy to love the people who think you're wonderful. It's difficult to love those people who think you're a jerk." Talk about telling it like it is! I don't always like to hear that—part of me wants to wallow in anger for a while. But Sande is always right to speak her mind.

So what did I do with the sweater? I took it back. I'm a frugal guy who can't imagine wearing something just once. I didn't want or need a sweater like that. I wanted something I could wear all the time. And I wanted something that my beloved bride would also like seeing me in. So why didn't she just come out and say she hated that sweater?

When we men ask a direct question like that—especially about cloth-ing!—we're looking for a direct answer. So do us a favor and save yourself the frustration. Simply say what you mean!

Just don't do it in the middle of the Super Bowl.

SAVE YOURSELF THE FRUSTRATION. SIMPLY SAY WHAT YOU MEAN!

You say: "Do you want to stop for ice cream?"

You mean: I'm craving a triple-scoop, hot-fudge sundae with one of those cherries on top right now, but I don't want you to think I'm a pig. Even if I have gained a little weight lately.

He says: "No, thanks."

He means: I'm not really hungry for ice cream right now.

You think: *What a jerk! I really need that ice cream . . . now. If he doesn't change his mind and pull over in two seconds . . .*

You say: "Oh, isn't that cute?"

> **You mean:** Hey, I'm thinking about where that might fit in our house. Maybe in the bedroom? No, that one corner is too crowded. But in the foyer, hey, that might work!
>
> **He says:** "Uh-huh."
>
> **He thinks:** *Oh, great, she wants to buy it. Don't we have enough stuff around the house?*
>
> **You think:** *Oh no, he hates it. And just when I figured out a great place for it too. Well, I'll just have to figure out something else to put in that spot. It'll look so empty.*

Shoot it to me straight!

Not only does he want you to say what you mean when he asks you, he wants you to shoot it to him straight. No emotion, no making him guess at nuances.

Here's another Leman family example.

Sande always looks so nice. She's always dressed perfectly for an occasion. When we go on a trip, she insists that she's packing light. But she brings one entire suitcase just for shoes because every outfit has to have matching shoes.

Then there's me—your oh-so-male kind of guy. I have a simple rule: inside shorts get changed; outside shorts you can wear for five to seven days. When we decide to go out to dinner with our kids, I'm ready in two seconds flat, because I don't have to change anything.

Sande takes longer. And when she sees what I'm wearing, she gives me the once-over. You know that look. She looks . . . most particularly, at my shorts.

I've known her for long enough to know what's going on in her head. I can see her weighing her words: *Do I really want to say something about those shorts? Is it worth it? Let's see . . . what kind of restaurant are we going to? If it's classy, I'm going to have to say something. But maybe that family place could be okay.*

Finally she reaches a decision. "Honey, how many days have you worn those shorts?" And I get the picture. Back into the house I go to change, so I'll be socially appropriate (though I can guarantee you that there will be other men at that restaurant who will have worn their outside shorts for five to seven days).

Or sometimes one of our kids starts in on me. (Wonder where they learned that?) "Dad, are you really going to wear those outside?" (meaning, outside the house).

So back into the house I go once again. I'm all about making my family happy.

But once I really blew it. I showed up at my daughter's school wearing my bedroom slippers, shorts, a T-shirt, and a baseball cap. I should have known by the look of horror on my 13-year-old daughter's face that I'd done something terribly wrong, but then I'm a male. I can be clueless sometimes. But did she tell me outright? No.

When I got home, Sande took the direct route. "You are never to show up at school like that again. It's important to your daughter."

I got the message. I didn't have to guess at any nuances because she shot it to me straight. She stated it quickly. She didn't drag out the facts, examine them 20 times, or make me feel like a bonehead.

I knew the case was closed. But I've never showed up at my daughter's school like that again.

You see, we guys are dumb as mud . . . but we are also very trainable. We want to please you. Because all of us are still little boys at heart, and you are the ones we look at with secret awe as the center of our world.

THE BEST WAY TO TELL HIM HE MESSED UP

1. Get him alone behind a closed door.

2. Touch him as you're talking to him. Because your guy is so touch oriented—and he especially likes to be touched by the love of his life—he's much more liable to pay attention to you. And the little-boy part of him will be saying, *Well, she's touching my arm, so she still likes me even if she doesn't like what I did.*

3. Soften his defenses by looking him straight in the eye and saying something like, "Hey, honey, I could be dead wrong/out in left field on this, but when . . ." Admitting up-front that you could be very wrong will make your guy relax, instead of feeling edgy or competitive.

4. Then slip him the commercial—what you *really* want to get across in a nutshell: "It seems to me that what happened today at lunch with your sister might have been taken differently than you really meant it. . . ." Explain what the other person (or you, if he hurt your feelings) might have thought. Remember that you are the relational person—that you have the advantage because you, as a woman, can see the "whole" of relationships much more clearly than he, as a man, can.

5. Always, always gently tell him when he messes up. Contrast that to, "Hey, Bubba! You really messed up! What is wrong with you? I can't believe what you said to your sister at lunch today. I was so embar-

rassed, and the people at the next table heard and rolled their eyes. You . . ." Such an approach will make your guy crawl into his shell and stay there.

The key is to always think, *If I messed up, how would I want to be approached?* Then give the same consideration and respect. The Golden Rule of Relationships is "Treat others as you yourself would want to be treated."

#2
THING HE'LL NEVER TELL YOU

"Think of me as a four-year-old that shaves."

Why boys never really do quite grow up . . .
and why you wouldn't want them to.

● ● ●

"WHY DON'T YOU GROW UP?"

"Yeah, just grow up!"

We seventh-grade boys stood in a tight huddle as the seventh-grade girls, hands on hips, defiantly hurled words at us. Evidently they thought we were acting stupid . . . when, really, all we were acting was like ourselves.

From the beginning of life, boys are . . . well, *boys.*

They make noises like *Vroom!* and *Urrrch!* And *Bbbppsssttt!* when they drive toy trucks and fire engines. They like to crash their vehicles, often at a top speed.

They whistle and spit.

They tease girls when they like them.

They burp at the dinner table . . . just for fun. We won't mention the other bodily noises that they work hard to make.

They face each other off in kindergarten with conversations like:

"My dad is bigger than anybody in the world."

"Oh, yeah? Well, my dad is bigger than your dad."

"You think so, huh? Well, my dad . . . "

They brag about their conquests . . . and who has a bigger appendage when they're in the shower at school.

And what happens when these little boys grow up?

The swagger and the risking spirit remain. Here's a case in point: the man who drives a pickup with this message in bold black type across his back window: *COPS LIE.*

As a friend of mine says, "Testosterone doesn't change when little boys grow up . . . because they never really grow up."

Within every man is still the little boy he once was.

WITHIN EVERY MAN IS STILL THE LITTLE BOY HE ONCE WAS.

YOUR BIG, LITTLE BOY

My mom hated doing my laundry, and who could blame her? One time she reached into my pants pocket and got bit.

"Keevvviin!" she screamed. "Get down here right now!"

From the way she yelled, I assumed somebody died. So I came running. "Yeah, Mom, what is it?"

"What is in your pocket?"

I shrugged and fished in my jeans. I pulled out a crayfish, a cricket, two salamanders, and a grasshopper. "Bait," I said proudly. "I went fishing today, remember?"

My mom probably wanted to strangle me, but she was a very patient woman. (I would prove to be the child who tested her patience the most.) She said, "Fine, but next time you go fishing, could you please remove all bugs, insects, and anything that's slimy and alive from your jeans before you put them in the wash for me to find?"

Then I went through my Milk-Bone stage. It takes a boy who watches his dog chewing on a Milk-Bone to think, *I wonder what that tastes like?* Worse, I found out I really liked the taste. Even more, I craved the attention eating the things brought me, and I took pride in doing goofy things.

My mom never got used to this trick, but other people have. One Christmas, a woman who heard me talk on the radio sent me a box of frosted Milk-Bone dog biscuits. If they had invented those when I was a kid, I never would have eaten my dinner!

It wasn't long until my 18-month-old son paid me back. I was in my office many years ago when I got a frantic call from Sande. She was crying—in near hysterics—and I immediately felt my heart start to race. I was positive one of my kids was dead or at least critically injured.

"Honey, what's the matter?"

"It's Kevin!"

Oh no! I thought. Aloud I asked, "Did he fall into the pool?"

"No," Sande said, "it's his pecker."

"His pecker?"

"Yeah, it's purple!"

"Purple? What happened? Did somebody hit him?"

"No, he colored it with a magic marker."

I burst out laughing. Little Kevin had always shown a predisposition toward art (art turned out to be his major later in college), but this creative endeavor really beat them all.

"What are you laughing about?" Sande asked, horrified.

"Little boys do things like that," I replied. "That's the funniest thing I've ever heard!"

Because all of us men were once boys, we tend to have a good laugh rather than a good cry when it comes to our own boys' childhood pranks.

Just because your husband has turned 30 or 50 doesn't mean he has lost his affinity for being a boy and doing goofy things. We might have learned to regulate it a little better, but many of us still surprise our wives with the seemingly senseless things we do. If you gave me a Milk-Bone dog biscuit today and I was in the right mood, I'd probably eat it (only Milk-Bone, by the way; no other brand will do!).

BOYS WILL BE BOYS

Boys never really do grow up.

It's why as soon as your husband's buddy gets a new two-seater, they peel out of your driveway to give it a spin around the block . . . and show up grinning three hours later when your pot roast is crispy.

It's why he can give you the grunt after work but then spend the next hour discussing with a buddy on the phone how to achieve all the levels in the *Call of Duty 2* computer game. It's why he doesn't see the broken faucet that needs to be fixed but knows the instant a new DVD is released at Best Buy.

It's why he gets the urge to put up a new fence in your backyard by himself when he sees a neighbor doing one.

Every man feels keenly within his soul "the constant search to be number one" that he is born with.

EVERY MAN FEELS KEENLY WITHIN HIS SOUL "THE CONSTANT SEARCH TO BE NUMBER ONE."

If you doubt this, listen to the difference between the way little boys talk, when they are carrying on a conversation among just boys, and the way little girls talk when they are carrying on a conversation among just girls.

Boys:

"Look what I can do!"
"All right! But I can swing higher."
"But I can hang upside down on the monkey bars."
"I can do that too. Race ya!"

Girls:

"Should we play house today? Or school?"
"Oh, why don't we play house?"
The girls look around the group, eyeing each girl in turn.
"Is that okay with you, Rachel?"
Rachel nods. "Sure, let's play!"
"How about you, Amy?"

Look carefully at each of the conversations. Are there any words that you see used repeatedly in the boys' conversation? What about in the girls' conversation?

Because of their drive to be number one—meaning everything else is secondary—little boys tend to use *I*. "Look what I can do!" Note also the inherent challenge: "Race ya." Boys are primed for independence, and that independent edge only grows stronger as they grow older.

BOYS TEND TO USE *I*. GIRLS TEND TO USE *WE* OR *YOU*.

Little girls, who are typically more relational in nature, tend to use *we* or *you*. They decide things by committee, getting everyone in on the decision and making sure everyone is okay with the next action before they move ahead: "Is that okay with you, Rachel?" and "How about you, Amy?"

It's no wonder that in marriage, it's important to you, as a woman, to get your guy's opinion of things that are important to you. But what you need to realize is that not everything that's important to you is important to him. Sometimes we men may not have an opinion because what you're asking about doesn't register high on our scale (more on this in chapter 3). Other times, our thoughts may be solidly mired in the muck of our own swamp, and we're feeling up to our neck in alligators. We may be worried that if we bail on a certain project at work, we may lose that job. And if we lose that job, what will happen to the house payment? the car payment? So your concerns—though important to men—may not rate as high as that drive to be number one.

Does it mean we men don't care? No, it's just that in the inner drive to be number one, all other things pale. That's why we may not remember, necessarily, something that you consider important.

It's because we have a strong drive to compete, and to every man, it's a dog-eat-dog world.

COMPETITION—THE NAME OF THE GAME

To say my wife, Sande, and I think completely differently about driving is an understatement.

She doesn't know to go to the outside lane and zoom around when traffic slows to a crawl in her lane. Instead she waits patiently in her lane to get to wherever she wants to go.

Then there's me. If there's even half-a-car-length gap in traffic in my lane, I'm zooming to the other lane to see how far ahead I can get. I even keep track of the guy in the blue pickup in the far lane, to see if I can get one up on him. And I can spot a handicapped license plate on a four-cylinder car a stoplight away.

Once when Sande picked me up from work so we could go out for dinner, she drove in the right lane and slowly pulled up to a stoplight behind a long array of vehicles, including a dump truck and a bus.

I took a quick look around. The middle lane had only two cars—both fast-accelerating ones. The outside lane had three minivans in it, so would probably be slower moving. The middle lane was definitely the one to be in.

"Uh, Sande, you might want to move into the middle lane."

"I'm very happy where I am," she said.

And she proceeded to stay there . . . in the slowest lane possible.

It was more than my competitive male ego could take. "You'll never win the race in this lane!" I exclaimed.

She gave me the look. The look all wives give their husbands from time to time. Then the classic line came next: "*What* are you talking about?"

It all comes down to the fact that boys are born competitive. They're determined to go after what they want. To duke it out when they need to.

If you doubt this for one minute and think I'm gender stereotyping, just watch two men play tennis, and then watch two women play tennis (unless, of course, the women are engaged in an Olympic sport). You'll quickly see the difference. Built within every man is the need to compete.

BUILT WITHIN EVERY MAN IS THE NEED TO COMPETE.

But girls? They are so different. In my career as an educator, I coached girls' basketball. I learned quickly that you don't yell at girls. You don't even raise your voice, or you might start a flow of tears.

One day a girl was wincing and crying and carrying on so much that I thought she had broken her wrist or her arm. When I raced over there, I heard through her tears, "Coach, I broke a nail."

Another time the game had already started, but only four of my players were out on the court. "Where's Brittany?" I ask, dumbfounded.

"She's in the shower, crying," one of the girls said.

While girls show their delicate emotions and frequently huddle in groups on the playground and discuss who's most popular and similar relational topics, the boys argue over who won the last competition. It doesn't matter whether they're playing a game of Monopoly, tossing around a basketball, or trying to stomp on and kill the highest number of ants. They usually want to be the best.

When boys grow up, they compare salaries and the size of their offices.

That's why it is particularly hard on a man when he feels inadequate in the area of competition. When he's lost in a midlife crisis or feels worthless because he can't hold down a steady job. When he feels his role in the home isn't really important (more on this in chapter 6). When he feels you could do just as well without him.

WHAT A MAN WILL NEVER HEAR OUT OF A WOMAN'S MOUTH BUT WOULD LIKE TO:

- "Why would I need more shoes?"
- "Hey, honey, I called the cable company today and ordered another outlet for our bedroom. I also ordered the NFL package and the hockey package. I hope you don't mind. That way you can watch as much sports as you want to in comfort."
- "I love it when you spend time with the guys. It makes me happy to see you happy and relaxed."
- "That new lawn tractor you bought is so cool. It's the biggest on the block!"

WHAT A WOMAN WILL NEVER HEAR OUT OF A MAN'S MOUTH BUT WOULD LIKE TO:

- "I've had enough sex for this month. Can we just cuddle and watch a romantic comedy tonight?"
- "I know this is a tough question, dear, but I want to ask anyway. What can I do to encourage your mom to stay longer than the six weeks she's already planning on?"
- "You just stay in bed and get your rest. I'd be happy to get up and take care of the baby."
- "Of course I know our anniversary is Super Bowl night. But I'd never dream of watching football with the guys on that night. You are first in my heart."

IT'S NOT JUST THE THING, BUT THE SIZE OF THE THING THAT COUNTS

To a man, it's not the thing that counts, but the *size* of the thing. It's why your guy gets an urge to buy a speedboat when his neighbor buys a rowboat. Or why he has to sign up to work out five nights a week at the gym when a coworker says he's going on Mondays and Fridays to tone up his abs.

Although you might roll your eyes at such bluster and swagger, it's all a part of that male competitive spirit. And it comes out in everything they do, even when they're supposed to be at play.

Ken, Jim, and Jason were "bonding over the barbecue" (as their wives liked to call it) one summer day and got a brainstorm: why not take one weekend in the early fall to go fishing?

Each made a note about the weekend on his BlackBerry, then promptly moved on to other topics.

The fall day before they left, they pulled together the rest of their plans as their wives looked on, amused at menus like

Breakfast: Steak
Lunch: Chicken
Dinner: Fish (They were evidently counting on catching some since nobody picked up any at the grocery store.)

There were no fruits, vegetables, or anything else from any other food group in sight. The men packed paper plates, but no knives, forks, spoons, or cups. There was no toilet paper, even though they would spend their time in the deep woods and on the river. The women all secretly wondered how their guys would manage over the weekend.

Two and a half days later, the guys returned home. They were muddy, disheveled, and smelling like fish. But all were beaming like little boys with their prize catches.

Ken had made a particularly big catch—a 50-inch muskie. Although the men had fried up their other catches, Ken had brought his muskie home wrapped in a plastic garbage bag loaded with ice to share with his wife, Andrea. And with little boy excitement, he displayed his catch before her wide eyes (and assaulted nostrils).

Three weeks later, Ken came home from work with a large box. "Just look!" he told Andrea.

There in the box was the muskie head, mounted on a memorial plaque, with the lure still dangling in its mouth.

"Isn't this awesome?" Ken said. "I can't wait to hang it up."

Ladies, guess where he wanted to hang it? In their bedroom, above the bed!

Andrea drew the line there in her mind. She couldn't imagine waking up every morning with that muskie staring at her. She had to stifle her urge to say, "Uh, what about the garage?" because she didn't want to deflate Ken's little-boy ego.

Instead, she wisely said, "You know, I've been thinking that we should turn the unfinished basement into a hang-out room for you and the guys. Would you be open to that? That would be a great place to hang that muskie—then you and the guys could remember your good time fishing together!"

Now that's a smart woman. Andrea understood how important not only the catch was to her big "little boy," but the *size* of the catch. Ken had competed in the fishing category with the other guys and won the biggest prize. Andrea was willing to make some adjustments that proved to him that what was important to him was also important to her. And she carefully sidestepped the issue of having that fish hanging over their bed.

By her quick thinking, she gave her big boy the stroke he needed. All because she understood that to a man, bigger is better.

> Marriage is a school where we learn to be flexible, to live in harmony with each other, to walk together as one, to strengthen and complement each other.
>
> —H. Norman Wright, *Seasons of a Marriage*

THE PRINCESS AND THE CONQUEROR SYNDROME

Most little girls long to be a princess. They dream of the arrival of a prince who will sweep them off their feet and away to a dreamy castle. They will live in perfect eHarmony in the land far, far away for the rest of their lives.

But what they often get is the "conqueror" treatment: "I am master of my destiny and yours, too, and I will rule over you." It's also known as the "cave man treatment"—"you woman, I man, you mine. You come to cave *now!*"

THE CONQUEROR

Every woman who has a guy in her life has no doubt lived through this scenario:

Man is driving the vehicle.

Woman is trying to sit patiently in the front passenger seat.

But as they circle the same block for the fourth time, woman gets itchy and speaks up. "Honey, could we be lost?"

"Oh, no," man says confidently. "It's just around this corner."

Ten minutes later they are still driving around.

"Honey, maybe we could ask for directions," woman suggests.

"No!" man responds vehemently. "I can figure it out myself. We're almost there."

Note the tone of the man's response. Why is he so annoyed?

To you it makes absolute sense to ask for directions when you're lost. After all, why spend all that gas and time driving in circles?

But look at it from a man's perspective. He is primed, as a little boy, to be a conqueror. That's why he doesn't appreciate even the *suggestion* of asking for directions.

In his mind, what you're saying is, "Uh, hubby dear, I think you're totally, impossibly lost, and you just don't want to admit it."

Your guy doesn't like feeling inept at anything because his inbuilt desire is to *conquer every task,* including ones he's not very good at. He believes that he can get the job done. Figure it all out for himself, without any help (including yours), thank you.

It is important to how he feels about himself as a male that you allow him not only to compete but to conquer.

So the next time you're in the passenger side and you're driving in circles, ask yourself, *Is it really so bad to let him try to be a conqueror? Even if it means driving in circles? or being a little late?* As exasperating as it might be to you sometimes, try to take the long view. Give your husband permission to try . . . and to fail, if needed. You'll get to your destination eventually, but you'll both be in a better mood if you let him be the conqueror he's designed to be.

Just remember: when you're driving and he's not in the car, you can stop a zillion times for directions with your girlfriends.

QUIZ

Why won't a man stop for directions?

    A. It's beneath him.

    B. He's got to figure it out himself.

C. He knows where he's going.

D. He doesn't like to ask others for help.

E. Because he doesn't have to go to the john yet.

F. He thinks, *I can still pull this off.*

For answers, see page 179.

Within every man is the need to conquer. That's why getting in the fast lane of life is so important. It's why having control of the television remote and being able to surf all the channels continually just to see what's on is so important, even when the constant clicking and switching of plotlines and characters drives you crazy.

There's another important side to the conquering man.

When he conquers, he conquers. In his mind, when he does the job, it's a done deal. Consider the man and woman who had been married for three years and were struggling in their marriage.

"But honey," the wife begged, "you haven't told me you loved me for three years!"

The man's response? Confusion flickered across his brow before he said plainly, "I told you I loved you when we got married . . . and that hasn't changed!"

In his mind, when he went through the details of the wedding and brought his bride across the threshold, he had conquered the marriage job. Then he was on to the next thing he needed to conquer— getting a higher-paying job to take better care of his new family.

Don't take your husband's singular focus personally. It's not meant to be directed against you (unless there's a problem in your relationship that he's trying to avoid). Instead, realize that your conqueror is conquering one task at a time. And at times he may need your gentle help to redirect or broaden that focus. (More on this in upcoming chapters.)

> TO A MAN, LIFE IS ABOUT WINNING. TO A WOMAN, IT'S ABOUT THE JOURNEY ALONG THE WAY.

THE CRAVING TO WIN

Every man gets up in the morning thinking, *I have to win. As soon as my feet hit the floor, it's a race for who gets there first, works the hardest, is the best, the fastest. That's the guy that's going to win. And it's going to be me.*

Although he won yesterday, it doesn't make any difference. He has to win again *today,* tomorrow, and each day after that.

You see, your man knows that, in today's world, there is no place for the loser. Your guy fears the downsizing of his company. He wonders if he'll be forced to relocate. If he stays with the same company, he'll have to take a pay cut. And that can't help but affect your life as a family.

Running constantly through his mind and his day is the thought that life is uncertain. Lives are changed with the stroke of a bureaucrat's pen. Competition is severe. Every day he faces significant pressure to be the best. To seal the biggest deal. To dig the foundation of a house faster than anyone else.

He has to win. And that internal thinking hangs over everything he does.

"I WANT IT—NOW!"

I'll admit it. Some days I have the maturity of a baby carrot. I crave immediate gratification. Kudos are important to me.

SOME DAYS I HAVE THE MATURITY OF A BABY CARROT.

A week ago, a woman walked up to me at a bookstore where I was signing copies of my books. After waiting for the crowd to clear, she said, "Dr. Leman, I've read all your books. But I want you to know that *Sheet Music* has changed my life, and my husband's and my relationship. We've struggled with sex since the beginning of our marriage. I never felt good about myself or the way my body looked. For the first time in 17 years, we're now enjoying sex. I wanted to thank you for that."

"Wow," I told her. "I feel like a seal that has just been thrown a big four-pound fish! Because this is why I do what I do!" That quiet kudo from a single woman meant the world to me as an author . . . and as a man.

Why were one woman's words so important? Because they told me plainly that my work counted. And to a man, that means *I count.* To a man, his work *is* who he is.

Contrast that to a woman, whose work is *a part* of what she does.

Remember in chapter 1 the two women who met over the punch bowl, and although both were working women, their occupations didn't even come up in their conversation? Such realities reveal the priority of work in a woman's life, even if she is a working woman—and even if she makes a large contribution financially to her family's bottom dollar.

In the pie of a woman's day, work is only one slice. It's why she will make phone calls during her breaks and lunch hour to make doctors' appointments and to check on ballet lessons, and she'll surf the Net for red Mary Jane shoes just because her daughter *has* to have them.

Because of a man's innate competitive drive, the urge to be conqueror, the craving to win, your man also craves *immediate gratification,* not down-the-road gratification. That means he wants to tell you immediately about a project he just nailed at work, and what his supervisor says about it.

Should a man always receive immediate gratification? No, because he'll become just like the boy who gets everything—a hedonistic little sucker who's impossible to live with.

But the wise woman realizes that a man is wired to want things *now.* And she will realize that a man who is constantly thwarted in his desires will begin to look for gratification elsewhere.

At times it may drive you a bit nutty to deal with your big little boy. The man who acts so competitive, like the conquering cave man, and who has to win. At those times, think of the situation with this little twist: If your guy wasn't so competitive, would he have had the guts to go after you? If he wasn't so conquering, would you have said yes to marrying him?

You see, you ought to be flattered. Your guy saw you as his prize to be won, and he went for it! He went for the gold—you!

YOU OUGHT TO BE FLATTERED. YOUR GUY SAW YOU AS HIS PRIZE TO BE WON, AND HE WENT FOR IT! HE WENT FOR THE GOLD—YOU!

THE OTHER WOMAN

Did you know that there is another woman in your husband's life? And that she's there to stay?

Often your husband's behavior has everything to do with that other woman in his life . . . his mother.

I am convinced that I am the man I am because of who my *mother* was.

"You mean your *father?"* you might be saying.

"No," I'd answer back. "Because of my *mother."*

After spending years in the field of psychology and talking to and/or counseling thousands of men and women, I am convinced that it is the father who makes the biggest difference in a daughter's life, and the mother who makes the biggest difference in a son's life.[1] These cross-sex relationships make indelible imprints.

I didn't grow up in a perfect family. My dad was a drinker. I didn't always have a good relationship with him. In fact, there were times in my life where I wished he was out of my life. But as I grew older, things changed for the better. I came to understand more about my dad and his own growing-up years that had impacted who he became as a man. His own Irish-Catholic family was so poor that he and his brothers used to say, "The first one dressed was the best dressed." That was because whoever got dressed first got the pick of the clothes. The other brothers got what was left over.

But I was always close to my mother when I was growing up. Even during the years when kids have a hard time talking to their parents, I could talk to my mother about anything—including girls and sex. My mother was always a straight talker. I knew she loved me. And, no matter what others said, she believed and expected the best of me.

Me. A kid who was dumber than mud in school. As a senior in high school, I took Consumer Mathematics—the class where you were presented with this kind of math problem: "Nancy went to the store with a dollar. She brought home four apples and 16 cents of change. How much did she spend at the store?" The class had a basic goal—to teach me how to shop at Safeway when I graduated!

Instead of a grade on my report card one year, there was a line there because I drove that teacher out of teaching. She left school in the middle of the term . . . because of me. I got thrown out of class. To this day I feel guilty for the way I treated that woman. I have tried on several occasions to find her to apologize face-to-face for being the kind of kid I was, but with no luck.

I received an incomplete even in that simple Consumer Mathematics class, flunked Latin three times, and never "got" chemistry at all.

Kevin Leman didn't look like he was on his way to any success in life.

After I became an adult, my mother once told me that she often prayed, "God, please have Kevin bring home just one C on his report card to show me there is *something* there." She was often at school more than I was—talking to teachers who were constantly saying, "If Kevin would only apply himself. . . ."

My mother had a lot of stresses in her life. We were poor. For part of my growing-up years, we didn't have a car. Instead my dad had a delivery van—the kind that had no seat except for the driver's seat. I remember sitting on the dry-cleaning bags and helping him deliver them to houses. We had a modest home that had been given to my father by an aunt.

> Love is optimistic.
> Love is tenacious.
> It keeps hoping.
> —Stuart and Jill
> Briscoe, *Living Love*

When my dad's business floundered, Mom picked up the slack, going to work full-time as a registered nurse so the Leman family could have the basics. She worked hard—often all night. One of my most vivid memories is of watching her walk through two feet of snow at seven o'clock in the morning. She was coming down our street in Buffalo, New York, after working the night shift at the hospital.

Because both my parents worked, I was a latchkey kid before it came into vogue. Everybody else seemed to have Ward and June Cleaver as parents. When another boy taunted me out of pure meanness, telling me my mother didn't care about me if she wasn't home when I got there, I knocked him back on his tail.

I loved my mother. And she clearly loved me and my siblings. In the midst of all the hard work, she would take time to go fishing with me. When I was five or six years old, we would walk to the creek, half a mile from our house, and catch fish. She would celebrate each of my catches as if it were the most spectacular catch anyone had ever made! My little-boy heart would swell with pride. Perhaps my mother already knew then that I would struggle academically and that I would need this kind of a boost early in life to be a success at anything.

Throughout my childhood, my mother was my champion. Even

when, in the world's eyes, I was a failure . . . and continued to be so for years.

After being thrown out of college, I spent nine months looking for the right job. I preferred an executive-level position, but the only job offered to me was as a janitor. It was a low point in my life, where the only badge I wore was the insignia of Tucson Medical Center house-keeping—a TMC and a crossed broom and mop—on my uniform. I was truly trying to "find myself." I decided to take a night course in geology at the nearby University of Arizona . . . and promptly flunked it. Someone told me that persistence pays off, so the next semester I took it again . . . and flunked it again. There I was, 0 for 2 at the university, floundering, and wondering what was next in my life.

But short of my twenty-second birthday, my life changed. I met Sande, a nurse's aide, and fell head-over-heels in love with her. When we started to date, she popped the question. She asked me if I wanted to go to church with her! You have to know that going to church was the last thing on my mind. My perception of Christians was that they were some of the weirdest people who walked this earth. But Sande had something that radiated out from her personality, and it attracted me. So I went to church with her that next Sunday morning . . . and then she wanted me to come back with her at night. I remember thinking, *No woman is worth this!*

But Sande was, so I went. That night the pastor talked about a guy who knew about Jesus Christ in his head but didn't know him in his heart. As I sat there, feeling very uncomfortable, I had to tell myself the truth: *I* was one of those guys, and he was talking about *me*. Every time I looked up, I saw the pastor's brown eyes looking right at me.

That evening I remember walking out of that church, feeling clean for the first time in my life. And I was in awe that I could not only talk to God, but that he would actually listen to me. I could have a *relationship* with the One who had made me.

The truth of the matter is, when I met God, my life did a 180.

In his mercy, he gave me motivation to go back to school not only for *one* class, but full-time, while I was still working full-time as a janitor.

That first semester back, I received all As and one B. I was even put on the honors list. I still remember staring at my name on that report card and saying my name audibly. "Kevin Leman." The grades were so incongruous with how I saw myself that I couldn't believe they were mine!

Soon after that I got a note that I was to report to the dean.

My first response? "I didn't do nothin' wrong!" (It was a learned response, believe me.) I was scared. My little-boy thinking told me, *Last time I saw a dean, he threw me out of college.*

I went to see him anyway.

"Son," the dean said, "you've won University Scholarship Honors. We're going to pay for your tuition next semester."

I about fell off my chair. Had I—Kevin Leman, flunky—heard right?

After that point, I became an honors student.

I had come so far . . . and I credit my success to my mother. She, of all people, was the person who had believed in me all along the way.

And that gave me the firepower for success in my adult life. It gave me the confidence to discover what I was good at.

I was so glad when at last my mother could retire. She deserved it. I wanted her to be able to enjoy life. After my mother died, I found a letter of mine she'd saved that I'd written when our daughters Holly and Krissy were four and two. Here's what it said:

> Sally [my sister] got the piano. Jack [my brother] got my train.
> But we really think we got the best thing:
> You in Tucson.

It was far more important to me—more important than any worldly possessions—that the woman in my life who had formed who I have become, could live in the same town and be a part of my own kids' growing-up years.

That "other woman" in my life made all the difference in the adult I am today. And your husband's "other woman" makes all the difference in the adult your guy has become.

SMOTHERING, DISCIPLINING, OR DRIVING?

The wise wife will take into account her husband's upbringing—the way he was treated by his mother, who had him for at least 18 years.

Smother mothers

Those who rock the cradle rule the world.

—Stuart and Jill Briscoe, *Living Love*

Smother mothers don't let their children play sports because they don't want them to get hurt. They don't want them to climb trees because they might fall. They won't let them go on hikes because they might get lost. In short, they won't let them do the things that boys enjoy most and that keep them competing, conquering, and winning.

Yes, those mothers might keep their children more "safe" physically. But there's a dangerous catch: If you keep a boy from doing healthy things for 18 years, he's going to rebel completely as soon as he gets the chance. He won't rebel by doing healthy things either, such as coaching his son's or daughter's basketball team or playing golf. Even worse, in many cases, the man won't be able to take it out on his mother, so he'll take it out on his wife.

Lucky you!

A smother mother often makes excuses for her boy. If the kid wants to duck out of school, she writes a note that says, *Seth is not feeling well.* If he runs off and plays before doing his chores, she shrugs. If he wants to play Nintendo instead of doing his homework, she looks the other way.

She is all too willing to "bend" the truth to protect her little boy's reputation.

Let's say the kids are late to school because Seth and Karyn were fighting all morning. The smart mom will put that bit of information in the note to school! She won't let the kids even *think* she'd cover for them. Instead, she'll write

Dear Teacher,
Seth is late to school because he was irresponsible this morning and kept fighting with his sister instead of getting ready.

The smother mother, on the other hand, will come up with a lame excuse that preserves her son's temporary "image" . . . but, in the process, she'll be sacrificing his long-term character.

Ever wonder why your husband might assume you'd cover for his mistakes? why you'd be okay with lying for him to save him from embarrassment? Take a look at his mother. Was she a smother mother? Was she his cover-up?

My kids know that I will die for them, provide for them, protect them, forgive them, and love them, but *I will never lie for them.* I won't make them weaker by allowing them to avoid personal responsibility.

> Before you flare up at another's faults, take time to count 10 of your own.
> —Mrs. Amos Miller

When a mother refuses to lie for her son, she's teaching him that women aren't for using. They aren't for hiding behind or to be used as part of a cover-up scheme.

If your husband's mom was a weak woman, your husband probably thinks that all women are weak, although he'd probably never verbalize it. If he learned early in life that he could control and manipulate his mom, he'll assume that he can control and manipulate you.

If you've married into this situation, what can you do? You've got to take charge. Right now. Lovingly but forcefully stand up for yourself and show some strength.

Another thing to consider is whether your husband's mom gave him room to fail. Once when I was on a radio program, a female caller said that in order for her son to get anything done, she had to follow him around the house, saying, "Pick up your shoes! Tuck in your shirt!" She went on and on about all the things her son never got done and the lengths she had to go to make him do them.

When she ran out of breath, I asked her, "How would you like it if someone followed you around the house with a pad and pencil, writing down all the things you did wrong? telling you, 'Clean that table again. I found a spot! Wash off the counter! Oops, you missed a piece of lint when you vacuumed the living room!'"

There was silence for a minute, then she said, "I wouldn't like it at all."

"Of course not," I told her, "and neither does your son. We parents mess up and kids do too. Don't hold your son to a standard you can't match."

We all need standards and principles, but I'm always suspicious of rules. When I think of guiding principles, I think of Jesus' approach to life: Love others as you would want to be loved. Love as I love you. When I think of rules, I think of the Pharisees' approach to life. You know, those nose-held-high-in-the-air and I'm-better-than-you folks in the Bible who were always "shoulding" everybody but themselves: "you should do this" and "you should do that."

I applaud parents who want to raise respectful, good-mannered kids.[2] But too many people in so-called Christian homes mimic the Pharisees more than they imitate Jesus. One of the key roles of being a parent is to temper your good intentions with grace. Moms, especially, can tend to be flaw pickers.

The law of the home should always be, Am I treating my family members the way I would want to be treated?

Enough said.

> Rules without relationship lead to rebellion.
>
> —Josh McDowell

A disciplining mother

The first mark of a disciplining mother is that she doesn't do anything for her kids that they can do for themselves. I'm not suggesting that a mother should refuse to serve her children a glass of milk when they ask for it. But have you ever gone to a science fair and realized that there were only one or two projects that were actually done by the kids, not by the parents? Some parents are so concerned with creating the *impression* that their kids are the best that they teach their children to put image over substance and display something that the kids know they didn't build.

If that child continues to place image over substance, he'll be all promise and no performance at work. He'll look like a devoted husband but may be anything but in his thoughts and actions.

If your husband's mother refused to participate in discipline, instead handing it over to her husband, chances are that your spouse doesn't take you very seriously. A child must develop respect early on, and the wise mom will use the value of shock to get her point across.

For example, if a son says something very hurtful—such as, "I hate you!" or swears at his mom—the disciplining mother won't fall apart.

Instead, she'll maintain her composure. But when that child comes to remind her later that day that he needs a ride to his basketball game, she'll calmly say, "I'm sorry, Billy, but you're not going to the game."

Billy is mystified. "What do you mean, I'm not going to the game? We talked about it this morning!"

"That's right, we did," she'll answer. "But that was before you spoke disrespectfully to me, which I don't appreciate."

Waiting until the right moment will create a shock value that will open this boy's ears. Dressed, ready to go out the door, he'll never forget this lesson. If your husband's mom caved in, however, your husband may treat your requests as irritations rather than something he should take seriously. This may be the time for him to experience some consequences of his actions.

The driving mother

Did your mother-in-law keep your husband busy, busy, busy?

I find more and more men in my counseling office who have no idea of what a socializing family is all about. Many of them never enjoyed leisurely meals at home with their parents. Instead of taking vacations with their siblings, they were off by themselves at sports camps.

The pace that some families set for themselves is crazy. I've talked to parents whose kids started tumbling and gymnastics when they were age three or four, soccer at five, T-ball at six, and karate lessons at seven. By age eight, they are doing all of those sports simultaneously in the same school year. I know of a 10-year-old boy—an only child—whose mom allowed him to play on three different basketball teams during the same season. That approach is plain nuts.

> The more busy you are, the more shallow you are.
>
> —Unknown

If your husband's childhood schedule included Scouts on Monday, basketball practice on Tuesday and Thursday, band practice on Wednesday, basketball games on Friday and Saturday, and youth group on Sunday, it's likely he didn't have a chance to really bond with his family.

As a result, when he marries, he may have a radically different view of what a family is and does. It may not match at all the image that you cherish of family togetherness.

Not surprisingly, he may bristle when you say, "Honey, we never see you anymore. Can we set aside at least two nights a week where we can have dinner as a family? All of us?"

Because such a picture has not been a part of his experience as a child, it will take some tricky finagling for you to "reeducate" him—in kindness and love, of course.

The most important thing is to remember that you didn't marry a "clean slate." Your man was shaped, formed, and molded by another woman. And that other woman—his mother—has made all the difference in who your husband has become today and how he relates to you and your children, if you have any.

But are you stuck with such behaviors? Certainly not! You, the one he loves and trusts the most, can make all the difference in your husband's life right now and in the future by how you strive to understand, accept, and celebrate him. See Manspeak for some starting ideas.

VIVE LA DIFFÉRENCE!

A big challenge in marriage is learning to understand someone who is so different from you (and I'm not talking just the interior and exterior plumbing).

> The goal in marriage is not to think alike but to think together.
>
> —Unknown

In today's honorable struggle to gain more respect for women, we've thrown out common sense with our prejudice. Clearly, men and women are of equal social value. Men aren't worth more than women. God doesn't love men more than women or women more than men. But society went south when it took this notion of equality and came up with this ridiculous conclusion: therefore, men and women are the same. And that's the message today's society—including advertisements and movies—tries to push.

But men and women are *not* the same. A man's brain and a woman's brain are different. For example, did you know that the part of the brain controlling visual-spatial abilities and concepts of mental space—skills necessary for tasks such as mathematics and architecture—is about 6 percent larger in men than in women?[3] Men's brains are larger, but women's brains contain more brain cells.[4]

Women's hearts beat faster than men's hearts. When men and women perform identical tasks, different areas of their brains light up in response.[5]

It's no wonder that a man finds a woman a mystery sometimes, and that a woman finds a man a mystery sometimes. We truly are different.

But I say, "Thank God, we're different!"

And as the Lord God said after he created Adam, "It is not good for the man to be alone. I will make a helper suitable for him."[6]

Then he created Eve.

I can picture Adam waking up to this beautiful creature by his side and his jaw dropping open in awe. And he probably said something very spiritual, like "Holy moley!"

As experts believe:

> The word *helper* may more accurately mean a *strength* or a *power*, and thus women are comparable to men. God, therefore, made woman for the man as his equal and his match as his partner in life. She was taken from *one of the man's ribs,* probably to show an interdependence. She was dependent on the man; men are dependent upon a woman to give birth to them. Some observe that the earliest language of Mesopotamia, Sumerian, has a word for *rib* that also means *life.*[7]

From the very beginning, God designed men to be men . . . and women to be women. And as such, we see life from completely different angles. Since you haven't ever been a boy, it's not surprising you don't think or act like one. And since your guy hasn't been a girl, it's not surprising he doesn't think or act like one.

But those differences, when taken hand in hand instead of as a competition, can lead to a most satisfying, exciting partnership.

A partnership where boys can be boys, and girls can be girls.

Even when both never quite grow up.

"MANSPEAK"

THE WAY TO WIN YOUR GUY'S HEART

1. Through your words and actions, take the competition out of your marriage. Focus on partnership, even if it goes against your grain.
2. Let him conquer. Even if you're not sure that he can do a particular task, let him try.
3. Don't feel or act slighted when he reverts to the little boy he once was. Remember: You're still the little girl you were.
4. Try to share his excitement over things that are important to him but may mean little to you.
5. Remember that *you* are the one he cares about the most. The one he worked hard to win.

WHAT DOES YOUR GUY NEED?

We guys really are simple. There's not much guesswork involved about what makes us clap our flippers and perform loyally for you like a seal at Sea World. If you understand our needs and throw us a few fish every once in a while, we'll be satisfied.

He needs to be babied once in a while.

When your man gets the flu or a cold, everything stops in your world. He needs orange juice every 15 minutes. He needs you to bring him the remote control, because he's too tired to move from his easy chair. He needs you to make him homemade chicken soup—even if you've never cooked any in your life and wouldn't know how. And he needs you to bring him that soup in a cup, with a straw, and hold it lovingly as he takes a sip.

Contrast this with what happens when *you* get sick with the flu or a cold. You drag yourself into the bathroom, pop a couple of DayQuil, and 20 minutes later you are going about your day as usual, accomplishing your huge to-do list for the day:

- Get dressed.
- Make hubby and kids breakfast.
- Make hubby's and kids' lunches.
- Write love notes for hubby and kids.
- Pack schoolbags.
- Check husband's color coordination. Send him back upstairs to switch clothing if needed.
- Kiss husband on his way out the door.
- Get kids out the door to the car on time and pick up other carpool kids.
- Drop off kids and speed to work for first meeting of the day.

The only time you stop to think about being sick is when you need another dose of DayQuil, and by then you need NyQuil.

Why do men become babies when we get sick? Because we revert to little boys who need someone to pay attention to us and take care of us. As irritating as it may sound, you morph in our minds from wife to mama. You're taking care of a little boy who needs to *know* he is loved by seeing it in action. He needs to know that he is a priority, and everything else is secondary to him (more on this in chapter 4). And that may mean putting your life and other priorities temporarily on hold.

He needs you to stop competing and let him win sometimes.

As annoying as it may be, especially to type A, driven women, there are times when you need to back out of the competition game and simply let your guy win. Yes, we are equal partners and helpmates. Yes, you have a brain. Yes, you may know how to do a particular task better.

But consider this: Because of his competitive nature, if you *always* compete with him, you're setting up a vicious cycle. And your guy isn't likely to back out.

Take this scenario, for instance.

Your husband pulls a stupid maneuver, and you're really ticked off. But you know he won't listen to your perspective because he never does, so you plot your next strategy.

In order to show him how mad you are, you decide to let his beloved pot roast cook a bit longer than usual (okay, an hour more than usual). Why pick burning pot roast as your symbol of competition? Because you know that good pot roast, done just right, is very important to him.

So what does he do? Stomp out of the house and go out for steak with a buddy. When he comes home late that night, he sees it as his right to ignore you, since you've been passive-aggressive with him.

Let me ask you: Is the cycle really worth it?

Have you ever seen the movie *The War of the Roses,* where Michael Douglas and Kathleen Turner play a married couple who play the competition game so viciously that they are left with broken hearts and broken lives?

Why not take yourself out of the game occasionally?

He needs you to let him be a boy.

Do yourself a favor and learn to laugh. Males do goofy things. We always have, and we always will. Nothing has changed since the beginning of time.

Even at the age of 47, we will still have muscle-flexing contests.

We'll decide to build a deck and be convinced we can do it in a weekend.

We'll stubbornly insist we can do things ourselves, and that we don't need anybody's help. Like the guy who spent three weeks agonizing over writing up job reviews for his nine employees . . . rather than ask his wife, who was a writer by trade, for help.

We'll make noises you'd rather not hear . . . and we'll make them more loudly when other boys are around.

We'll laugh too loudly.

We'll embarrass you by wearing plaids and stripes next to each other.

But how much of that "little stuff" really matters in the long run? After all, we put up with you during that lovely time of the month when your personality is far from charming.

When he's being a boy, why not reflect instead on what attracted you to him in the first place? List all his good qualities. Post them on the mirror for him to see. He may not say anything about the list, but you'll see his chest puff out with pride that you're pleased with him.

One of the top things on my wife's list was a man with humor. She's certainly got that!

YOUR GROWN-UP BOY AND HIS BIRTH ORDER

As simplistic as it may sound, I am convinced you can tell a lot about people by their birth order.[8] As you seek to understand your guy—to anticipate his needs, fulfill his desires—it helps to know how he was raised. It makes a big difference whether your spouse was the leader of the pack or the baby of the family. And it helps to know and understand yourself too! And it all starts back in your husband's family, when he was a little boy.

Firstborns

Firstborns or only children are achievers or overachievers and are usually scholarly. Because they are the first, they are in a precarious position because there are so many pressures on them, but many handle those pressures beautifully and do amazing things. Only children have even higher standards for themselves than firstborns.

For instance, of the first 23 astronauts the United States sent into space, 21 were firstborns. The other two were onlies. Accountants, engineers, computer programmers, architects, doctors, and attorneys tend to be oldest children. What do you suppose Queen Oprah's birth order is? Or the blue-eyed wonder Phil Donahue? Or Dirty Harry, Clint Eastwood? The only comic I know with a doctoral degree, Bill Cosby, is a firstborn. I suppose we should really call him William. He gave all his kids names that start with the letter *E* so they would remember excellence. George Bush, Bill Clinton, and numerous other presidents and municipal leaders are firstborns—natural leaders.

No surprise, because the oldest child is not only an achiever, but ordered, well-disciplined, and well-organized. Since a firstborn's parents are new at the child-rearing business, they tend to overreact to this child. Every dirty diaper is cause for alarm, and every step is cause of rejoicing. Because parents are learning, they tend to be inconsistent in their

FIRSTBORNS ASSUME THAT IF THEY CAN'T DO EVERYTHING, THEY ARE WORTHLESS.

behavior. They try one thing, and if that doesn't work, they try something else. As a result, the firstborn may become fearful and apprehensive because he doesn't really know where he stands.

But they are also in an enviable position because they have their mothers and fathers to themselves for a time. They get a lot of attention early in life. That's why firstborns tend to be very tuned in to adult values and feel more comfortable dealing with adults. They tend to be dependent upon the family—meaning they will uphold the family values and that approval of the family is important to them.

A firstborn is an achiever, reliable, conscientious, cautious, and conservative. He is likely to be a hard worker, a good provider, and someone who sees that all the needs of his family are met. He is also likely to be a perfectionist and competitive by nature. It will help him get ahead in his career and provide well for his family. But he can also view your marriage as a competition rather than a partnership. And when he fails at a task, he can get really down on himself.

If your husband is a firstborn or an only child, what can you do?

- Let him know that you aren't interested in competing with him.
- Tell him that you appreciate his accomplishments.
- Encourage him in his dedication to succeed.
- Show through your words and actions that you view your relationship as a partnership, not a competition.
- Let the little boy within shine in front of others since that is important for him.
- Encourage him when he fails—and give him another chance.

If you are a firstborn, rein in your competitive urges. Let your husband "be a man" and take the lead once in a while. And when your own perfectionism kicks in, take the long-range view.

Middleborns

Middleborns are the ones literally "stuck in the middle." The firstborn has already paved the road with the parents; now the middle one slides into the family and has a role model and an instant playmate. Because they are in the middle, they make very good peacemakers and negotiators. They make friends easily and are loyal. They're the child with the thinnest photo album.

As a whole, middleborns are the most faithful marriage partners. They don't let stress get them down, but they attack problems with gusto to get them settled. They don't let conflict remain in a family for very long without talking about it and trying to resolve it. And being in the middle, they have a lot of training in give-and-take.

But because a middle child is good at compromising, he may be hesitant to tell you what he really thinks, even when you ask. He may say, "Oh, it doesn't matter that much" when it actually matters greatly. If you're married to a middleborn, you have to watch carefully to make sure you're not trampling his feelings. Because he is so susceptible to peer pressure (what others think of him), he may tend to do things to make you and others happy.

If your husband is a middleborn, what can you do?

- Model for him that you really do want to hear what he thinks . . . that you value his input.
- Make sure you don't judge his opinion when he does share it with you.
- Assure him that he doesn't have to do something he doesn't want to do (or buy something he doesn't want to buy), just because someone else is doing it.

If you are a middleborn, realize that your viewpoint is just as important as anyone else's. Take the risk to speak up so that those who love you won't have to play "guess what she thinks."

Lastborns

Lastborns are the ones forever showing off.

He's the one less likely to be spanked or disciplined by his parents. He tends to get away with murder and goes laughing his way through life. (I am a good case in point.) He isn't the most responsible, dependable fellow. He loves to get others to do things for him by appearing helpless or charming and is very good at it (he's had lots of practice at this as the baby of the family).

Because a lastborn is the youngest and smallest, everyone helps him, whether he needs it or not. So he often heads into marriage with some ideas that life will be fun and easy, and there are no consequences to his actions. After all, his parents were easier on him because, frankly, they were plain worn-out from raising all the other kids! A lastborn is used to having things his way, doesn't like anything uncomfortable, isn't very disciplined, and isn't into achievement. But he's charming, happy, fun-loving, and spontaneous. And he loves to be the center of attention.

If your husband is a lastborn, what can you do?

- You may need to give him a nudge in the right direction to encourage him to help you pick up the house and to be accountable for things he says he'll do.
- Gently keep an eye on his impulses (such as spending too much on a new toy). You will have to be the one to say, "Can we really afford this right now?" And then you'll have to prove to him that you can't.
- Talk through consequences of a particular action before your spouse goes ahead and does it.

If you are a lastborn, realize the most important thing to do is think and evaluate before you do something you'd normally do spontaneously. A little discipline and a plan of action wouldn't hurt!

WAS YOUR MOTHER-IN-LAW A . . .

Smother Mother?
- Was she afraid that her little boy would get hurt?
- Did she make excuses for him? bend the truth to protect his reputation?
- Did she give him room to fail—or did he have to be perfect?

Disciplining Mother?
- Did she not do anything for him that he could do for himself?
- Did she create a true picture of what he was like?
- Did she discipline him when he needed it, or say, "Wait 'til your father gets home!"?

COMBATTING "THE OTHER WOMAN"
The other woman—your husband's mother—is here to stay. No matter your view of her, she has influenced your husband greatly. If you understand how, you'll understand your man even better.

The smothering mother
If, as a youngster, your husband was held to a standard by his mother that he could never fulfill, he is going to react somewhat explosively to your corrections. You might think it's a minor thing to point out that the mirror he hung is a bit crooked, but what does he hear?

"You've messed up! You're an absolute failure! Can't you do anything right?"

I know you don't mean to convey this impression, but because of his rearing, that's what your husband hears. You're a woman, and right now, you're sounding an awfully lot like the mother who harangued him for years. It's no wonder you get the stiffened back, the pout, the angry frown, or the silent treatment.

In a man's mind, there are no degrees of success—only pass or fail. But here are two great ways you can ask for some self-improvement of your guy without setting off his sensors of a performance-based self-worth. They won't happen overnight, but they're well worth the work.

1. Brag about not only what your husband does but who he is—right in front of him! Let him know that you appreciate the character qualities his mother might have missed and that despite some of his shortcomings, you're delighted with your "catch." You'll need to be consistent and persistent because you're working to overcome 18 years or more of negative training.
2. Add some sugar to your corrections. For instance, you could say, "That looks Terrific, honey. You've put the mirror exactly where I want it. It's so good of you to get that done. I wonder, however, if it might be a little crooked? Do you think that's a problem, or is it just me?"

BRAG ABOUT YOUR HUSBAND—RIGHT IN FRONT OF HIM!

The lack-of-disciplining mother

If your husband's mom caved in under discipline and just said, "Wait until your father gets home" whenever her son did something naughty and disrespectful, you have a challenge on your hands. Your husband may treat your requests as negotiable rather than something he should take seriously.

When you remind him that he'll have to pick up some cash at the bank after work if he wants to go to a movie with the guys, and he gives you an irritated, "Yeah, I know," don't bail him out when he comes home without the cash—even if you have a secret emergency stash.

If he whines about being late to meet the guys, don't rescue him. Don't make his problem your problem. Don't accept his irresponsibility as your responsibility.

Don't call to reschedule appointments for him. If the appointment is for him, and he can't make it, he ought to be the one rescheduling it.

If he forgets to bring his paycheck home two weeks in a row, serve him a bowl of cereal with no milk for breakfast the next morning. When he says, "Hey, where's the milk?" you can quietly say, "There's no more milk. I couldn't go grocery shopping yesterday, because our account is low. If you bring home your paychecks, I'll be able to go grocery shopping tomorrow while you watch the kids."

Keep the tone of your voice level and nonaccusatory. Simply state the facts that are the result of his lack of follow-through.

It may take a few times, but after a while he'll get the idea that you're not his mother, and you're not going to pick up his responsibilities where he dropped them.

The driving mother

Do you wonder why your husband can't slow down? why he always has to keep moving, keep working, and even playing hard as if he were working? Let me provide a clue. Chances are, his mother kept him busy, busy, busy. Although this lifestyle is also true of many young women, parents naturally drive their sons a little harder and often keep them a little busier. Maybe it's because, underneath it all, they hope keeping a boy busy will keep him out of trouble.

If your husband was born with a type A personality and has been programmed to be driven, I'll be honest with you. You're going to face a lifelong battle getting him to slow down. What you *can* accomplish, though, is slowing him down by degrees.

The responsibility for such a life change will, however, fall on you, because you are more of the relational one in the marriage equation. And it takes work to maintain a healthy, happy home. Here's what I mean.

IT TAKES WORK TO MAINTAIN A HEALTHY, HAPPY HOME.

One December, an editor was visiting us. Our son, Kevin, was home from college, and Krissy and her husband, Dennis, came over too. It was one big, happy, Leman family reunion. After watching how close our kids were and how much they enjoyed being together, this editor asked me, "How do you raise a family like yours?"

"What do you mean?" I asked.

"How do you build a home where everybody wants to be together?"

"It's all about bonding," I replied. "The Lemans have never been big joiners. If our kids had traveled three different directions five or six nights a week, we'd never have had time to bond as a family. But since we severely limited outside activities, we spent—and still spend—lots of time together, which is why our family members want to be together today. We actually *like* each other."

Whether you have children or not, the principle is the same. How many nights do you spend running to activities? How many nights are booked with time away from home? away from your guy and any other family members?

If your husband grew up with a driven mother, you have to save him from himself. He'll run himself ragged (and you too!) if you let him. He needs you to put on the brakes, redirect his energy, and keep him focused enough so that he can concentrate on the things in life that really matter.

Like your relationship.

You can't compete with a mother's upbringing, but you can work around it.

And when you choose to do so, I'll give you a guarantee. Yes, you'll have some short-term struggles. But the long-term results will be a happier, healthier home life—and more satisfied partners.

#3
THING HE'LL NEVER TELL YOU

"I have a purple dining room, and I could care less!"

Why a man's home is really not his castle, and why you're tempted to turn him into a girlfriend.

● ● ●

IT'S TRUE. I have a purple dining room, and I couldn't care less. And when I say "purple," I mean really purple. Even the walls are purple. At first when my wife told me it was going to be purple, I raised an eyebrow. But I'm used to it now.

It's an absolutely beautiful room. If you stepped into our home, you could tell that my wife is one of those ladies who loves looking through home-decorator magazines (she has a stack next to the bed that you wouldn't believe), because she put a lot of original ideas together when we built our house.

You have to walk through an arch to get into our unique, eight-sided dining room. It has real hardwood floors (not the press-it-onto-the-floor-in-one-night variety) and an arched, eight-foot-wide picture window that looks out onto the creek that circles our house.

The room is marvelously decorated in "shabby chic"—as Sande would call it. The antique table is made of oak, with beautiful leaf patterns on the sides of it. Right now, as I walk through the archway into the room, I see eight chairs around the table (it changes from day to day, depending on what our kids are doing and who is visiting), but there are another six chairs in the room. An antique chandelier with one of Sande's handmade wreaths graces the ceiling above the table, and candelabras light the walls. There are a total of 34 candles in the room (I counted once for fun). Two china cabinets with mirrors beautifully display Sande's eclectic treasures.

It's the kind of room where every woman who walks into it stops, looks around in awe, and exclaims, "Oh, it's so beautiful!"

That's my wife. She has a flair for making things beautiful. That's her thing.

But you know, I wouldn't care if the room were all orange. If she announced over dinner that she was going to paint our front door a combination of purple, pink, and red, and give it a barn theme, I might roll my eyes a little, thinking, *There she goes again.* But it wouldn't really matter to me.

My thinking regarding a door extends this far: *Will the door keep rain and snow out? Good. Then it's functional.*

When you get right down to it, the color of my dining room or door isn't what matters most to me. I care about how comfortable my bed is, how big the bathtub is (and whether a Jacuzzi is involved to ease my stress at the end of a long day); I care about my car, my dog, Rosie, and my bank account. What I do each day is governed by what comes in on the fax machine from my assistant, Debbie. She's the one who tells me what I'm doing today, tomorrow, and next week—what deadlines and interviews I have.

So why would I care whether or not I'm sitting in a purple or an orange dining room?

You see, there's a big lie going around. It declares boldly, "A man's home is his castle."

Oh no, it's not. It's the woman's. The man just lives there. Why not call it like it is?

WHY A MAN'S HOME IS NOT HIS CASTLE
1. The only real dominion he has is the garage.
2. All the stuff he bought by himself for his home somehow makes its way *quickly* to the garage.
3. He doesn't spend much time in the inside of the castle because he's afraid to sit in the "for décor only" chairs.

4. His main responsibility at the castle is cutting the lawn and removing the dog plops resting there.

5. He doesn't even know what the color mauve is, and even if he did, he's color-blind anyway.

EVEN NOAH GOT NAGGED . . .

I live in the hills of western New York in the summertime. One of my daily treats is listening to John and Denny, two talented DJs who bring life to Family Life Network radio stations through their portrayal of funny vignettes based on the Bible. They'll take all kinds of Bible stories and delightfully present them, but one in particular caught my attention.

They were talking about Noah, the man in the Old Testament who built an ark. He did it because God told him there was going to be a huge Flood that would wipe out everything on earth. But because Noah was a righteous man, God wanted to give him a chance to save himself . . . and his family.

Poor Noah. Day after day he worked, building that ark. He had a hard time of it. With all that hauling, cutting, and hammering of wood, he was exhausted. The hecklers made things worse. Every day they'd come by and watch his progress on the ark. They'd shake their heads, scratch their beards, and laugh. "He's nuts!" they'd say, pointing and waggling their fingers in the loser sign.   .

One day, when patient Noah had nearly had it with all the naysayers, his wife showed up at the work site. "Hello, up there!" she yelled up the gangplank. "Noah, what color of curtains do you think we should have in the ark? Should they be blue to match the ocean? Or maybe yellow to match the sun? What do you think?"

He barely looked up from his work. All he called back was, "Honey, whatever color you want it to be is fine."

And he went back to building his ark.

She continued to press. This time she walked up (uh, no, *stomped* is more like it) the gangplank. Her form blocked the sun, so Noah couldn't see to work any longer.

Her hands were thrust on her hips in what he knew was her exasperated stance. "Well," she said, "what color are you going to make the door? If I don't know what color you're going to paint the door, I don't know how to coordinate the curtains."

All poor Noah said was, "Honey, whatever color you want it to be is fine."

As I was listening, I nearly drove off the road because I was laughing so hard. Here was poor Noah, trying to save himself and his family from drowning when the big Flood promised by God came. And what was on his wife's brain? Color coordination!

I could relate. Especially since Sande and I had built our house just a few years earlier. As God is my judge, I never looked at the plans for the home after it was designed. When Sande asked me what I wanted, I told her, "I want a big bathtub and a big bedroom. If you give me that, I'll be happy with anything else."

I know there are men who might want to be involved with the decoration of every nook and cranny of the house. In fact, we know one couple like that. She's a stay-at-home mom of four children, does all the finances, orders the phone service, and mows the lawn. He's the one who chooses the wallpaper, creates beautiful stained-glass lamps from garage-sale bases, and recently designed a jungle bedroom for their son. But that makes sense—he's a designer!

For most men, however, the colors of the curtains and the dining-room walls aren't that big of a deal. One man told his wife, "I don't care what color you make our bedroom—as long as it isn't pink." What did his wife, a pink-and-ruffles kind of gal, choose? Shades of mauve and wine. Her guy was fine with that because it wasn't the one shade in the world he hated—Pepto-Bismol pink. It never entered his brain to think, Hey, aren't mauve and wine a shade of pink?

If Sande changed the shade of purple on our dining-room wall or painted it a completely different color, it might take me weeks or years to notice unless she chose to enlighten me regarding it over dinner. However, I'd notice immediately if she moved the remote control four inches to the left!

Can I state the man's rule of thumb on decoration simply?

"If it makes you happy, it makes us happy."

Most of us men wouldn't have a clue what the "color wheel" is or how to use it.

Yet you ladies insist on trying to get us involved in the decoration process. You say you want our opinion about the way the house should look. But we're not fooled. We can tell you already have yours formed.

Shall I say it again? A lot of marriages would be in better shape if you women realized, "If *you* are happy, then *I* am happy."

Right now, as I write this, Sande is on the phone in our purple

IF *YOU* ARE HAPPY, THEN *I* AM HAPPY.

dining room. She's calling a landscaper to see if they can plant some flowers and bushes at our house.

I see a slight frown on her face; then she asks, "Well, do you have anybody who is more of a designer?"

I can bet the guy on the other side of the phone is saying, "I thought you just wanted some flowers and bushes planted. What do you mean by 'a designer'?"

I shake my head. We live in Tucson—a hot, dry place. Everyone knows nothing grows here. Most people have given up. But not my wife. Every year Sande insists on planting bushes . . . and they die due to excessive heat in late spring and early fall.

To make things worse, in the wintertime, it's actually 10 degrees cooler at my house than it is a mile up the street. Not great conditions for keeping any flowers or bushes looking healthy.

But here's what is most funny to me. Sande is asking for a *designer* when the holes are already there. *So,* my male mind says, *what exactly is there to design? You just bring the live bushes and dump them in the holes. That seems simple enough. Why would you need a designer for that? You only need a guy with a wheelbarrow and a few muscles!*

However, I know my wife will prevail. She will somehow find a "designer" who will help her color coordinate our bushes. And when he arrives, she'll be out there directing his color-coordination process. After all, I'm convinced from living at my house that she has more design ability in her little finger than many designers who do it for a living.

The frugal (a nice way of saying "Leman, you're cheap!") side of me winces. I realize those bushes, once again, will look pretty for a few months. Then they'll wither and die. Just like the ones the year before . . . and the year before that . . . and the year before that.

But because I love my wife, I've decided not to make this little molehill into a mountain.

To put things simply, I gladly acknowledge my wife's foibles and live with them since I've got some of my own. And I realize that, to

BECAUSE I LOVE MY WIFE, I'VE DECIDED NOT TO MAKE THIS LITTLE MOLEHILL INTO A MOUNTAIN.

her, making our house look pretty is a priority. So even though that is not my highest priority, I am happy when planting bushes every year makes her happy.

"If *you* are happy, then *I* am happy" is an easy rule that suits more occasions than just home decoration.

THE GIVING DISEASE

Sande and I are both givers. But the way in which we give is very different.

One Christmas I worked at a Christmas tree lot. I watched as couples and entire families came to pick out their trees and left with the "perfect tree" in tow. Then a father and his young son arrived. They walked the entire lot, but I noticed that the seven-year-old kept returning to one particular tree. It was the most expensive tree on the lot. I saw the discouraged look on the father's face as he trudged over to the son one more time and told him in Spanish, "Son, we can't buy that one. It costs too much."

The son was determined. He stayed his ground, right beside that tree, and replied to his father in English, "How much does it cost?"

I stepped up. "Well, you're in luck," I said in a jovial tone. "That tree only costs a dollar. We've been trying hard to get rid of it all week!"

I took that father's dollar, and when they walked off the lot, I paid the cashier the difference. *After all, if you can't do something like that once in a while,* I thought, *what's wrong with you?*

As Jesus said, "Freely you have received, freely give"[1] and "Give, and it will be given to you. A good measure, pressed down, shaken together and running over, will be poured into your lap. For with the measure you use, it will be measured to you."[2]

But my wife, Sande, has the giving disease really bad. What my heart was moved to do on the tree lot doesn't hold a candle to what she believes. Her entire life follows the proverb "The righteous give without sparing."[3]

Sande used to own a shabby-chic antique store called Shabby Hattie. People loved that store. It smelled like lavender, and her clients could buy lavender by the scoop . . . the old-fashioned way. When she wrapped a present for somebody, she would wrap it so well that the person didn't even want to open it. Every package got a scoop of lavender, crinkly paper, and a bow on top . . . all for free. And every person who entered her store got a gift—a lovely silver pen—whether they bought something or not.

One day, after seeing several of those pens walk out the door with customers while I was waiting to pick Sande up, I was brave enough to ask her, "Honey, how much do those pens cost?"

"Oh, not much," she said and proceeded to drop a scoop of lavender into the package she was wrapping.

I pursued my goal. "Honey, *how* much?"

"I told you not much," she replied with a hint of irritation.

> The best relationship is the union of two very different people, who are good appreciators.
>
> —Unknown

Okay, so now I was evidently *sounding* like a man, and Sande had surmised—correctly so—that I was on the trail of this particular line of conversation.

I finally wangled out of her that the pens cost 15 dollars apiece.

Fifteen dollars!? My heart nearly went into overdrive.

It was one of those times when I wondered, *Can't you take just a little break in giving away the family farm?*

Then there was the time when Sande went to a baby shower at church. A young woman had become pregnant and didn't have the benefit of a husband. So Sande bought several outfits for the baby and attended the shower.

When she got home, she told me, "Leemie, I still would like to send that young woman a couple hundred dollars. She really needs it."

Again, I reined in my frugal nature. "That's fine, honey. Go right ahead," I said.

Why didn't I blow a gasket? Why didn't I give her a lecture about how we could use that money for something else? Why did I tell her to go ahead? Because *that is who my wife is.* She's one of those rare people in the world who have the gift of giving.

Sande also has the tremendous gift of making anybody feel like the most important person in the world. I wish I had that gift, but I don't. She's truly unique.

And I, of all people, have benefited the most from that gift. There's a reason why Kevin, the baby of the family who failed at many things and needed to feel important, needed to marry a woman of such quality and character as Sande. God knew exactly what I needed and sent this treasured woman my direction.

So who am I to say now, after we've been married all these years, that she can't give to others in the way God prompts her to? that she can't give just a little but in an overflowing way? If I didn't allow her and support her, I would be hindering her from being the woman God created her to be.

QUIZ

If he cleans the entire house and offers to take you to Talbot's to buy you a few outfits

> **A.** he just bought a new set of golf clubs for way too much money.
>
> **B.** he cheated on you.
>
> **C.** he realized this morning that your anniversary was in February and not in May.
>
> **D.** he thinks you need a little sprucing up.
>
> **E.** he's hoping to get lucky tonight.

For answers, see page 180.

A LITTLE SECRET ABOUT YOU WOMEN

Here's a little secret about you women. People and relationships are what register highest on a woman's scale. It all goes back to your three highest needs:

1. affection
2. honest, open communication
3. commitment to family

A woman defines herself as part of a family. If the family isn't working, she feels like a failure. If her house is a mess, she feels like a failure. If a friend is angry at her, she feels like a failure. If her husband doesn't go to a social event with her, she feels incomplete because he's not experiencing it with her.

Let's say your husband has been late coming home from work for three nights in a row. What's your first response? Instead of saying what we men would say, "Yup, he's got a big project brewing, and he's gotta get it done," what's your first instinct? *Maybe he's upset with me. What did I do that he doesn't want to come home until so late?*

PEOPLE AND RELATIONSHIPS ARE WHAT REGISTER HIGHEST ON A WOMAN'S SCALE.

Let's say it's been one of those crazy weeks where you've spent extra hours at your quilt shop, one of your kids got the mumps, and your refrigerator went on the fritz. At the end of the week, you stand, hands on hips, surveying the wreck of your kitchen, living room, and dining room. What would we men say if we looked at it? "Okay, so it's a little messy, but think about the kind of week you had. When on earth would you have had time to clean?"

What's your first instinct? *I can't believe I let it get so bad. What a mess! I just can't get it all done! What's wrong with me? How does Sue do it with four kids and working full-time? I only work part-time!*

Let's say your husband got the flu right before the big fund-raiser banquet, so he can't go with you. What would he say? "Sorry, honey. Bad timing for the flu, huh?" (But inside he's thinking, *Well, hallelujah. If I had to get the flu, this is good timing. I hate those fund-raiser banquets.)*

What's your response? "Oh, honey, I can't believe you're so sick! Should I go or stay home with you? It won't be the same without you there by my side."

A LITTLE SECRET ABOUT US MEN

Here's a little secret about us men. Things are what register highest on a man's scale. It all goes back to his three highest needs:

1. to be respected
2. to be needed
3. to be fulfilled

A man defines himself *apart from relationships* and identifies with things. That's why sports are important to him, and competition is important to him. It's why you see so many guys driving around with guns mounted on the backs of their trucks. (For guys, remember, it's not only the thing, but the *size* of the thing that matters.) It's why he can easily wave off social events and say, "You go ahead and go. I'll stay home and putter in the garage."

But what do most women think of that response? *Oh, he doesn't really mean that. If I get him to go, he'll enjoy it.* (More on this phenomenon in chapter 6). Why do you respond this way? Because women need men present in order to complete their happiness in the experience. Most men, on the other hand, would rather be somewhere else.

Ron once rescheduled his entire business trip so he could be home on a Friday night when his wife was having some neighbors over for dinner. By the end of the evening, though, he was stumped about why it was so important for him to be there. He spent the whole night washing dishes in the kitchen, wondering, *Why did I even bother to rearrange my trip?* Yet at the end of the evening his wife told him, "It was so great for you to be here." She hadn't even seen him, but she *knew* he was there. And that made all the difference in the world to her. The success of that dinner party, in her eyes, hinged on whether or not he shared the experience *with her.*

So let's be frank. Because of the vastly different needs of a woman and a man, a woman defines herself around a man, but a man doesn't define himself around a woman. If you don't understand that key difference, your feelings will continually be hurt. If he says no thanks to a social engagement or doesn't show up on time to something you've agreed to do, you'll think, *He doesn't need me! He doesn't love me! I'm a failure at being a wife!*

It's like Todd, a guy we know, who had only been back from his honeymoon for a day. After work, he headed home and sat down to watch TV. An hour later his mother showed up, eyed him with a frown, and said, "Uh, aren't you supposed to be home—with Melissa?"

Todd had forgotten he was married and had gone to his "other home." His *parents'* home. By the time he walked through the door of his and his bride's one-room apartment, her face was tear streaked, the "first dinner together" that she had lovingly prepared was ruined, and he spent the rest of the evening trying to make up for his forgetfulness.

"Don't you love me?" she asked, sobbing.

"Of course I do!" he said, hugging her.

"Then how could you forget to come home to me?"

How could he say that he had forgotten because he was a male, had a one-track mind, and it wasn't tracking in the direction of his lovely young bride right after work? that he had just done what came naturally to him? what he had done for years before their marriage?

WHAT YOU WON'T HEAR A MAN SAY

"You know what I like best about my wife? She's one tough guy and can give you a good karate chop."

WHAT YOU WON'T HEAR A WOMAN SAY

"You know what I love best about my husband? He's so incredibly effeminate."

HE'S NOT YOUR GIRLFRIEND

It can be annoying to deal with someone who is so different from you. But did you marry a guy—or a girlfriend?

As odd as this may sound, many a woman spends her marriage trying to turn her husband into a girlfriend. The kind of person she can shop with, have coffee with, gab with, share every detail of her day and her emotions with, enjoy romantic movies or fine-arts plays with . . . the list goes on.

But as good as that sounds initially, is that really what you want? A "girly" man? One who will giggle with you over the latest fashion statements? *Ooh* and *ahh* over that cute pair of white shoes with large rhinestone buckles? Empathize with you ad nauseum over what a coworker said and how it hurt your feelings?

There are some things that girls need to share with girls, and guys need to share with guys. Just because you enjoy something doesn't mean you have to do it with your man.

For example, there are few movies that I like. So I always tell Sande,

"Go with your girlfriend Teri and have a good time." Then my buddy Moonhead and I get lost by ourselves doing something we enjoy. Like going to stock-car races and inhaling the exhaust fumes. Something Sande would *never* enjoy. In fact, she'd be horrified by all the toxic fumes that we are sucking into our bodies and stupefied by all the noise. It would not be on her radar screen for enjoyment.

If you want to see a chick flick, get your girlfriends together and go see one. Let the guys go see the latest tough-guy film together. Or allow your husband the gift of staying home.

It's all about allowing each other to be who God created you to be individually. Being joined as one doesn't mean that your uniquenesses disappear. It doesn't mean you blended into a boring oneness, that you'll never disagree, and that your interests became his interests and vice versa. My Sande is an engaging conversationalist, a sweet wife, and a lovely hostess. But she's got her idiosyncracies. She likes her back scratched in an S shape. Her idea of packing lightly for a trip is to have only *one* suitcase that's all shoes.

> Let there be space in your togetherness.
> —Ralph Cansler

But she is the woman God has given to me, and I wouldn't trade her for anything. Even with all her quirkiness, I would never want her to be like my buddy Moonhead. I really *like* my buddy Moonhead, but I sure wouldn't want to be married to him!

I enjoy the surprise—the mystery—of the feminine touch. So does every guy. Even if that means a purple dining room.

But you wouldn't find me, as a guy, going out of my way to keep that purple dining room in tip-top shape.

Then there's Sande, the queen of the castle. One night last week I reached over to touch her in our bed and she wasn't there. *Odd,* I thought, waking up fully.

I squinted at the clock. *1:45 a.m.* What was up with that? Where was my lovely wife?

I dragged myself out of the bedroom, listened for any sound, looked for a light on, and found signs of activity in the dining room. I found her there, standing on a chair, meticulously cleaning and decorating the chandelier with a flower swag!

As a man, I enjoy our house looking nice. I deeply appreciate all that Sande does. But you would *never* find me up at 1:45 dusting and decorating a chandelier . . . or anything else that has to do with a household task. The only ones up in the neighborhood were the raccoons and my wife.

Clearly, there are differences between men and women. Differences in priorities. I see them every day between Sande and myself. You see them every day between yourself and your man.

But those differences are what make life as a couple exciting, fun, and well, yes, unpredictable at times.

And I love it.

Even if my home isn't *my* castle.

It's hers, and that's what makes her happy.

In the long run, it's what makes me happy too.

Man: "I'm the rooster, and I rule the roost."

His buddy: "Yes, but she rules the rooster."

"MANSPEAK"

TWO GOLDEN RULES TO KEEP THE TARNISH OFF YOUR MARRIAGE

1. Let boys be boys.
2. Let girls be girls.

WHEN YOU FIRST MET YOUR MAN, WHAT MADE HIM FASCINATING? Was it the fact that he did everything like you? Doubtfully. Show me two people who are exactly alike, and within a couple hours they'll be in football gear, bashing helmets and growling at each other. If you agreed on everything, you'd have an incredibly boring life.

Instead of letting your differences create tension, enjoy them. Laugh over them. Let your guy be who he is. You be who you are. Enjoy those differences between men and women.

I'm certainly not the king of good taste, but I can tell when people put a lot of time and effort into decorating for an event. Take, for instance, what women do for a get-together. They color coordinate the plates, forks, and cups. They bring in special tablecloths. They make centerpieces. They place little handmade favors by each place setting. And then, for extra fun, they mount a winning ticket under someone's chair. That person gets to take the centerpiece home.

Contrast that with a male event. I belong to a group called Man to Man. We men meet at 6:00 a.m. and have a "devotional" time, for lack of a better term for men. The pastor of my church leads it. How do we prepare for this event? We show up, whack off a hunk of brown butcher paper from a nearby roll, lay it over a table, and dump a bag of bagels and a box of Krispy Kreme donuts in the middle of the table. For our centerpiece, we add a tub of butter 12 inches in diameter with a king-size knife stuck in the middle. In two seconds we're done not only with our decorating, but we've got the food groups covered as well. The ambiance is wonderful.

SOME THINGS YOU JUST HAVE TO LET GO . . .

Many of the things your husband does may seem downright crass, socially inappropriate, dumb, a waste of time and money, or purposeless. But if you love him and it's important to him, you can choose to let those things go.

Another case in point about my giving wife.

When two publicists phoned to say they'd like to talk with me about my latest book, they said they'd like to take Sande and me out to dinner.

Great! I thought. *I'm all for free dinners.*

Not Sande. "I'll make dinner here," she insists.

Why? I'm thinking. *If we have them over for dinner, you'll have to work hard. You wouldn't have to. They're willing to take us out for dinner. What's the big deal? Why not give yourself a break?*

But I don't say that aloud to my dear wife. I know better.

All that day she works hard to make a special dinner. And it's one of my favorites—pork tenderloin.

As we're walking the two publicists out the door later that evening, all of a sudden it hits me. *They didn't get "the gift"! What's up with that?*

Then just as we reach the antique gate, Sande says, "Wait a minute. There's something I forgot." She zooms into the house and comes out, a minute later, with two little bags full of homemade treasures . . . one for each guest.

I can't help but grin inside. That's my Sande. Any evening at the Leman house is not complete without this gift-giving ritual.

Although my male head says, *This gift-giving business is so stupid . . . and expensive,* I realize that because I love Sande and respect her, I have to go along with it. I have to help finance it. Even when it makes no sense to me.

When you think about your guy, what things does he do that seem like a waste of time, money, or purpose? Does he buy the guys at his shop donuts every Saturday morning? Does he set aside Thursday nights to race radio-controlled monster trucks with a buddy in a store's empty parking lot?

Have you ever considered exactly what those activities are accomplishing in your man's psyche?

Giving donuts may be the one thing he can do that's within your family budget that makes him feel good about "providing" for the other guys. It might even make him feel like a hero.

Racing monster trucks may be his time to hang out with a buddy who is going through a divorce and having a rough time of it. Do they always talk about the divorce? No. Do they ever talk about the divorce? Oh, yes. Even if it's only in 30-second intervals. Thursday nights are the one time these two good friends are one-on-one and can risk opening their hearts . . . even if it's in the midst of a monster-truck testosterone fest.

When your guy does things that annoy you, how do you respond? How will you respond now, in light of this new information?

What activities is your loved one involved in that are good for him—even if they annoy you sometimes?

THE "DO EVERYTHING TOGETHER" FALLACY

Often a woman, being a relational person, has a fallacy firmly cemented in her brain: *Once I am married, I'm supposed to do* everything *with my spouse.* And she proceeds to act on that fallacy every day in her relationship with her husband. He's clueless about what feels to her like a marriage rule. All the while he's thinking about his dog-eat-dog world and trying to escape to the one place where he's allowed to be alone . . . the bathroom! See why you and he clash sometimes?

> To love someone is to affirm that he is worthy, to bid her to live life freely, to leave him with all his freedom intact, to recognize her dignity as a person, to invite him to grow, to oblige her to be fully what she is, to inspire him to be all that he can be.
>
> —Pierre Teilhard de Chardin

Couple time should be a priority in your relationship (more on this in the next chapter, in fact). But does this mean you have to do *everything* together? Absolutely not! Boys need boy time; girls need girl time.

My wife loves to shop. Recently she and a friend were talking about how wonderful it would be to have a "girl" outing.

She reported the conversation to me.

"What would you do on this outing?" I asked.

"Well," Sande said excitedly, "we'd shop, have a treat, go out for lunch, shop some more, then go to a movie, then shop. . ."

I got the picture. I love my wife, but I can do without all that stuff. Shopping is not my bag—no pun intended—but I know it's important to my wife.

So I tell her, "Go and have fun!"

By now she's been married to me long enough that she knows she'll have a happier Leemie on her hands when she gets home from shopping if she goes by herself or with a girlfriend.

For her sixtieth birthday, I wanted to give Sande something special. So I surprised her with the gift of going to Paris and London for 10 days with a friend. "Go, honey, and have a great time. It's my gift to you!"

I assured her I'd be fine. I would stay home and be Mr. Mom.

But when I drove her to the airport, I cried (literally). It would be the first time in 38 years of marriage that Sande and I took separate vacations. I really missed her while she was gone, but I also felt good about what I had done. It was an entirely unselfish gift. There was no agenda, nothing in it for me at all. I truly love my wife and was not trying to get rid of her.

She had the time of her life. It was a vacation she will always remember with joy. And I remember it with joy because I made my wife happy.

The next time you get annoyed at something your guy wants to do

1. Consider what the activity is. Riding his bicycle with a group on a Saturday morning? Planting a garden? Skiing in Colorado? Having a twice-a-year guys' only weekend?
2. Make a list of what this activity will accomplish for your guy. How does making this list change your perspective?
3. Instead of being jealous that you can't be part of the event or sad because you can't do everything together, support your husband in his endeavor, if at all possible. You'll have a happy, satisfied hubby as a result.

THE TRADE-OFF

Set aside some time to reflect on the following questions. Even better, go out for coffee or take a walk with your guy and discuss them together.
1. What things do you and your man like to do together?
2. What activities do you and your loved one do separately?

3. What is the trade-off for each of you in those activities?
4. What gifts has God given to your guy?
5. What gifts has God given to you?
6. How do these gifts complement each other in your relationship?

WHY NOT PLAY THE TRADING GAME?

Sande loves the Festival of Carols in Tucson. I hate it.

It's a Christmas program of music that's 14 tiers above the "Walking in a Winter Wonderland" variety. Really classy music. The program and the singing go on forever, in my opinion. Add to that the fact that in an auditorium, I'm not comfortable unless I can sit in an aisle seat, and sometimes aisle seats aren't available. I guess there are a lot of guys who are also dragged to this event every year who are taking up those aisle seats, hoping for a quick exit.

Every year, Sande buys tickets to this event, and every year I go with her. I know it's important to her enjoyment of the event to have me there. You see, there's a trade-off. I sometimes go to events I don't enjoy but Sande enjoys because it's important to her.

And Sande sometimes does activities with me that she doesn't enjoy, but she goes because it's important to me.

Football games, for example. Part of my enjoyment of going to University of Arizona games is having Sande with me. Usually we go with our friends Joe and Teri. It takes the edge off an event that otherwise would bore our wives to tears. (One time, in fact, Sande got so bored that she *lay down* on the bleachers during the game. Understand that she's five-foot-nine-inches tall, okay? But she just stretched out on the bleachers!) To Sande and Teri, a game is a social event, a gab fest, a time to enjoy each other. To us guys, it's a no-talking event. In fact, Joe wears headphones and I wear headphones and we sit together.

Our conversation goes like this:

"Ahh!"

"Ooh!

"Kill him."

"Get him."

"Stop him!"

Then a sigh of disappointment.

At halftime we talk a little bit and, because we've ignored our wives for half of a football game, we turn into doting husbands who ask our wives politely what they would like to eat and drink. We march up the stairs and bring back assorted goodies for them. I think they know they've been scammed but, nevertheless, both put up with us with joyful hearts because they know how important it is to us for them to be there with us, even though we ignore them and don't talk with them.

Couple time should be a priority in your relationship, but that doesn't mean you have to experience it the same way. For example, I love to fish. I love to be with Sande. So combining the two is my kind of heaven.

To Sande, going fishing with me means she can lay out on a boat and read girl magazines and sun worship. "Honey, look what I caught!" I'll say happily, and she'll give me a sleepy "Uh, huh." I know she could care less about the fish, but she gives me the verbal strokes I need anyway.

The point is, we're together, but we're enjoying the experience differently, and in a way that suits both of our needs.

I always laugh and say it's like the manatee and the slug. And that's the truth. One time while we were fishing Sande fell asleep on one of those floating rafts and literally floated out to sea. I had to flag down the water-rescue guy to go get her!

The moral of the story? You can do things together as a couple, but you don't have to do the same things. Sande can sun worship and read magazines while I fish. We're still on the boat together . . . except when she's floating out to sea, that is!

What do you do together happily as a couple—but do differently? How does that satisfy each of your needs?

#4

THING HE'LL NEVER TELL YOU

"I'm desperate for you to need me."

Is your guy starving for attention . . . from you?

● ● ●

MAC'S A SALESMAN who has been working hard in the tool-and-die industry for over 20 years. Each year there is an awards dinner in January, and all the sales reps travel to one location. They spend two days in meetings at a hotel, then get to "play" the third day, all expenses paid. Best of all, the top regional salespeople receive awards.

Usually the company frowns on bringing wives along on these trips because they won't pay for them, but this time the company encouraged Mac to bring his wife, Ginny. They also told him he was going to receive the award for top salesman in his region. That meant he was one of four top salespeople in the nation. He had come so far since the beginning, when he was scratching for even one sale.

When Mac found out the meeting would be held this year in Orlando, and that the company had booked him a $625 luxurious Class A suite, he began forming his plan to surprise his wife.

The next day he phoned the Orlando hotel and arranged for flowers to be waiting for Ginny in their room. He left work over lunch to shop at his wife's favorite store for an outfit he knew she'd love to wear to the awards dinner. And he bought her a new nightie, as well as her favorite Godiva chocolates.

He was getting set up not only for a great time away from his business but a little "just you and me, baby" vacation with his wife. He had *plans.*

He thought about those plans through that week and into the next, when he and Ginny headed to the airport, luggage in tow, and boarded the flight to Orlando. He was still thinking about those plans and what he would do in what order, and hoping the hotel folks didn't mess up on the flowers, when he and his wife opened the door to their beautiful suite.

It was perfect. The flowers were there in all their glory—all red, just like he'd ordered. His wife's favorite color. *Plans are proceeding nicely,* Mac thought.

He was unpacking his suitcase to begin the next step of his plans when his wife's cell phone rang.

"Oh, great! You're here already!" she exclaimed. "We're in suite 212. Come right on up."

Here? Who's here? Mac thought. *And why are they coming up?*

Unbeknownst to him, Ginny had phoned their two daughters, who both attended a nearby university and had their own apartment. She'd told them about the Florida trip and had invited them to come and stay with her and Mac at the hotel.

Talk about throwing a wet blanket over Mac's romantic plans! After 21 years of marriage, business stresses, and meeting the needs of the children, he had been looking forward to celebrating his successes at work with his wife . . . alone. It was the first time ever that he would have been able to combine business and pleasure.

How did he respond? He hugged their girls, but then grew quiet and withdrew emotionally from the conversation. He listened for a while as the three women talked and laughed. Then he walked out the door, strolled down the hallway, and was gone for two hours.

"What is wrong with you?" Ginny wanted to know when Mac returned to the suite. "Why are you being so grumpy?"

She had no idea why he was acting the way he was. . . .

Mac was desperate for Ginny to need him—*just* him. When she included others, his plans for romance were short-circuited. He first grew quiet, then withdrew, then became passive-aggressive. *Well, if she doesn't need me, then I don't need to be here.*

Theirs was not the getaway either of them had hoped for.

HUMPTY DUMPTY SAT ON THE WALL, HUMPTY DUMPTY HAD A GREAT FALL . . .

We men don't like to admit it, but we are as emotionally fragile as Humpty Dumpty. We know we're supposed to be tough guys, so we try hard to look like it on the outside. But on the inside? One little push sends us tumbling over the wall to break in pieces on the other side. Especially a push from the woman we love the most. And when we fall off that wall and get broken, sometimes we can't put ourselves back together again.

It all comes down to this in your guy's thinking: If you don't need me, if others can replace me, why am I beating my head against the wall? Why do I spend 10 hours a day at work? travel so much? eat bad food? drive over an hour in traffic each way to get back and forth from work?

Remember a man's three basic needs? To be respected, needed, and fulfilled? If those top needs are met, not only will he be happier, but so will you.

Men have a lot in common with cocker spaniels and golden retrievers. They all need to be stroked. And if you stroke them, they will reward you with loyalty for a lifetime. Their eyes will not wander to anyone else. They will come trotting happily to your side as soon as you call.

That's because, to your guy, you are the one who matters most when the rubber meets the road. You're the one who captured his heart, the one he chose to love for a lifetime.

That's why it hurts him so deeply when your attention is diverted from him and on to other things. He wonders, *I guess I'm not very important to her anymore, huh?* What self-respecting man would want to stick around if he's not feeling respected, needed, or fulfilled?

As Proverbs 13:12 says, "Hope deferred makes the heart sick." It creates emptiness and bitterness.

There's another way Ginny could have handled that business trip that would have satisfied both parties. Because she wanted to enjoy some time with her two daughters, she could have said to Mac, "I can't wait to enjoy two whole days and nights with just you. I'd also like to see the kids, if that's possible. Could we stay there one more night and ask the girls to join us?"

Once Mac had exercised his plans, he would be one satisfied customer. Like a chimp sitting on a bed made of bananas. And you know what? He would have been glad to see his daughters that third night!

But notice what comes first. First is the two nights with the love of your life. Then the kids would be allowed to come on the third night.

When Holly and Krissy were four and two, Sande and I took a short little vacation together. We left the kids in good hands with their grandma. All the while I was thinking, *Free at last! We get to go to California, spend time on the beach, have nice dinners. Just the two of us.*

What a wonderful time we had! The first day I didn't talk about the kids at all. The next day I found myself talking a little more about the kids. By the third day, Sunday, when we had to hop in the car and drive home, guess what? I couldn't wait to see the kids! They were now a priority in my mind because I'd had a great time with my wife. I'd had her all to myself for a while.

If you want your husband to love your kids and not regard them as competition for your time, you have to find time for just the two of you. The day is coming when your kids will be gone. But your husband will remain. Don't lose your place in his heart.

It's a lie that only women need intimacy. Your man is crying out (silently) for intimacy. But he does it in a very different way than you would.

THE MALE DEFENSE
Instead of telling you verbally what he needs, your guy is most likely to behave in one of the following ways when he is feeling dissed:

1. Get quiet or withdraw (like Mac did first).
2. Sulk.
3. Act passive-aggressive (Mac's second stage of defense).
4. Act like a four-year-old (as we talked about in chapter 2) and throw a mini temper tantrum.

Kay and Seth married when they were both in their thirties. Both worked full-time for the same company, so they carpooled to work.

They ate lunch together every day, and made dinner together. They had a schedule for their evenings that worked like clockwork for them, and looked like this:

Monday: Work out together at the gym.
Tuesday: At home night.
Wednesday: Couples' Bible study.
Thursday: Have dinner guests over.
Friday: At home/snuggle/movie night.
Saturday: Make breakfast, catch up on laundry and housework in
    the a.m. In the p.m. do something fun together, like a picnic in
    the park, a piano concert, or a visit to the arboretum.
Sunday: Church and rest day, nap.

Five years later Seth II came along, and their clockwork schedule was blown sky-high. Both agreed that Kay would stop working outside the home, and they would tighten their budget.

Seth assumed that because Kay was no longer working, she'd still have time to do all the things she did before—write love notes to put in his lunch, bake homemade cookies, and that their evenings would look pretty much like they used to, except a third little person would be added in the bassinet at their side.

Seth tolerated the first month of their disrupted schedule. He assumed it was just a "transition time," and soon Kay would have this motherhood stuff figured out and could get back to her regular tasks.

But the next month proved to be the same. Seth would arrive home, and Kay wouldn't have even started dinner yet. Seth was a "have dinner promptly at 6:00" kind of guy. He'd get quiet, withdraw to change his clothes, then shuffle into the kitchen to start dinner as Kay sat in the rocker and breast-fed the baby.

Two more months went by. Both parents now knew what "sleep deprivation" meant, and it wasn't a joke. Seth Jr. was a colicky baby. Kay spent her nights soothing him, so wasn't often awake when Seth had to leave for work.

Seth started to sulk. He acted like the injured party.

What is wrong with him? Kay wondered. *Doesn't he know how exhausted I am? And what I spend my days doing? I can barely get myself out of bed in the morning. All my energy has to go to the baby right now. He can't change his own diaper or feed himself, can he?*

Two more weeks went by. Seth would come home now and *stomp* off to their bedroom to change his clothes before plunging in to make dinner. Every time he had to start dinner, he would bang the pots and spoons and slam drawers shut as if to say, *Look at all the things I'm doing for you!*

Kay knew that not having dinner ready bothered her husband, but it wasn't like he was a Campbell's soup kind of guy either. And opening a can was about all she could manage in the midst of the exhaustion and busyness of her day.

One day, wanting him to know how much she loved him, Kay skipped her much-needed catnap so she could make a real dinner. She envisioned how pleased Seth would be at smelling the roast, carrots, and potatoes in the oven when he came home.

Unfortunately, right as Seth's car pulled into the garage, the baby threw up . . . all over the clean outfit she had just put on and her hair. As the goo dribbled down her cheeks, the door opened.

Seth took one look at her and exploded. "What is wrong with you? Can't you even get yourself cleaned up for me?"

To state it mildly, Seth threw a temper tantrum. He acted like a four-year-old. All because he was starving for his wife's attention. He'd known what it was like to have it fully, and now he felt completely deprived of it. He was not a happy camper.

Just a minute! you might be thinking. *What a jerk! What a loser! I'd like to kick him from here to tomorrow. It's exhausting to be a new mom. Doesn't he get that?*

> Marriages may be made in heaven, but people are responsible for the maintenance work.
>
> —Unknown

No, frankly, he does not. He's not a woman, and he has not birthed a baby. He doesn't know how exhausting it is to take care of a helpless child's needs every minute of the day. By the time he got home from work, the baby was awake for only an hour. When the baby did wake up during the night, his wife took care of the child. (Men can't breast-feed, after all.) Seth might wake up for a minute; then he was sound asleep again.

So when he walked through the door each day, he was thinking,

Hey, this parenting thing isn't so hard. So what's her problem? How come she doesn't pay attention to me anymore?

By now you might be a little ticked at Seth, and rightfully so. Seth is a little more immature and selfish than the average male, but we all have our moments.

WHAT A MAN IS REALLY SAYING WHEN HE ACTS LIKE A BABY

As annoying as the male species can be, it's important to try to look beyond our behavior to the clues of what we are really saying.

"I need you to pay attention to me . . . *now!*"

Behavior like Seth's may seem incredibly childish to you, especially when you're running crazily from moment to moment, trying to accomplish so much . . . and often your running is on behalf of children who can't do things yet for themselves.

But consider this: A woman is an expert at diversion. Let's say your two-year-old is playing with something she shouldn't have. The smart mom will divert that child's attention. Because that method works so well with children, she's also tempted to use it with her husband.

> Marriage isn't a sole proprietorship; it's a partnership.
> —Unknown

Let's say that you've just combed your hair, brushed your teeth, and fine-tuned your makeup. You have on a silk blouse so you look really good for the committee meeting this morning. Then your husband comes up and embraces you from behind. The kids aren't around (or you don't have any), and you can tell he's interested in a little playtime.

"Not now," you protest, "I have to get out the door. I'll see you tonight." And you whiz out the door, leaving behind a frustrated love-of-your-life because your DayTimer has too much on it for the day.

What does he think? *There's no room in her world for me.*

"I'm jealous of the time you spend with the kids. There's no time left for me."

Your jaw may drop at this one because it's so out of the realm of your experience and emotions, but it's true for men.

To a woman, when a man spends time with their children, he's spending time with her, because children are an extension of their mother. That means when her husband loves their children—wrestles with them, plays with them, reads to them, rocks them—he is also loving her. It goes back to the relational needs at the core of a woman.

CHILDREN ARE AN EXTENSION OF THEIR MOTHER.

I tell this story at marriage seminars, and it always gets an *Ahh* from the ladies. When my daughter received flowers and knew they came from a Leman, she immediately assumed they had to be from her mother. "But Dad, when I found out they were from you, that was even better!"

"*Ahh* . . ." the ladies in the audience always say.

"Did you hear that *ahh* in the audience?" I ask the men.

There are grins and chuckles from the male population.

"Well," I say, "each woman is dying to give *you* that *ahh*. Whenever you do sweet, manly, sensitive, gentle, loving things for your daughter and show that side of your nature to her, you are also doing those things for your wife. Did you know that?"

And the lightbulb goes on in the guys' brains.

A woman lives by this adage: "If you love me, you will love the people dearest to me and treat them well."

When a father shows that kind of love and attention to his daughter, you think, *Wow! I am so lucky to have married that man! Boy, did I choose right!* All of a sudden, you are feeling more romantically inclined toward that man.

But this is not so for the man. For a man, children are a separate entity. He doesn't emotionally connect them to the mother. In a very real sense, because he identifies more with things, he sees them as things (no offense to the children) that compete with him for your attention. And boy, do they compete! Children are hedonistic little suckers who will take all the time and attention you can give them . . . and then some.

It's no wonder they drain you of energy and leave you too exhausted to take care of the big boy in your life, the hedonistic big sucker who, from time to time, also needs all your time and attention and then some.

"Dr. Leman," you're saying disgustedly, "are you saying I should placate my husband when he acts like a child? I mean, he's a grown-up, for Pete's sake, and a father now. Shouldn't he act like it?"

Let me counter by asking you, "Do you placate your children at every turn?"

I hope not, because they are prone to think only of themselves. If you placate them at every turn, they'll become unionized and really work their advantage.

Husbands can be the same way.

The main point I'm trying to make here is that you need to realize that the role your children play in your husband's life is different from the role they play in your life. Until you do, you'll be making your husband's jealousy—or potential jealousy—worse.

FOR A MAN, CHILDREN ARE A SEPARATE ENTITY. HE DOESN'T EMOTIONALLY CONNECT THEM TO THE MOTHER.

"I feel like I can't do anything, and I'm not really needed."
I will never forget holding my granddaughter, Adeline, when she was six months old. Her mommy had handed her to me, and I felt so privileged to hold her. For a second, she looked at me as if she was going to cry. (Yeah, I know. I can look pretty scary sometimes.) Then her eyes landed on her mommy, standing right next to me, and I saw peace come into her expression. Her mommy was there, so everything was going to be all right. Although she knew my face and voice, they were not as familiar as her mommy's. And if she had to chose, you bet she would choose Mommy.

This kind of behavior makes sense, since children are attached to Mommy from the minute they are conceived or adopted, and they are nursed and most often fed by Mommy.

This can leave new dads feeling a bit out of the loop. They're helpless—often they can't help feed the baby. Or if they attempt a feeding, the temperature of the baby food or formula is a few degrees off from what the mother would do, and the baby starts yelling out of frustration.

What happens next?

"There, there, little one," Mom says and sweeps in to take over.

Within seconds the baby quiets down and magically all is right with the world again. The "fix it" person is there.

How does that make us men feel? Relieved, yes, but also frustrated at how inept we are in this situation.

If a man doesn't have an understanding wife who says things such as, "Oh, honey, he's been fussy all day. Thanks for trying. I really appreciate that . . . and you. I'm hoping to get him to bed a little early tonight so we'll have some uninterrupted time for a change. Could you help me by putting the dishes in the dishwasher? That way we'll both be done about the same time, and we can relax together."

THE POWER OF A WOMAN'S WORDS TO CHANGE A MAN'S FEELINGS AND PERSPECTIVE IS INCREDIBLE.

The power of a woman's words to change a man's feelings and perspective is incredible. You hold your man within the palm of your hand. Suddenly, with those few words, he can feel much better about his role in the family.

In that short scenario, you'd told him that

1. You think he's done his very best in helping with the baby.
2. You're trying your best to get some uninterrupted time with your big boy because he's important to you.
3. You've given him a task that makes him feel helpful and good at something, even if he doesn't have this baby thing down yet.
4. You've told him you *need* him and his help.
5. You've said that you are looking forward to time with just him.

You'll be amazed how eager your husband will be to get not only those dishes put away but to clean up the entire kitchen too.

After all, the person he looks the most forward to having time with is *you*. And I'm not just talking about when you're in the sack. You're the only one he truly wants to be intimate with.

But sometimes it's so hard to get to you!

TRYING TO DO IT ALL

One of the most difficult things about being a woman in America today is that everybody wants a piece of you. Your boss wants that memo. The church is looking for "only one" evening a week. The kids want to get to three different locations, all within the same hour. The teachers want a homeroom helper. Of course, to save up for the kids' college tuition you're also running a Mary Kay business on the side.

Because you're great at multitasking and you are relationally oriented, women will always find themselves juggling a much larger scope of tasks than men will. But if you are too busy climbing the corporate ladder, running an at-home business, or carpooling the kids everywhere, your relationship with your man will be the first one to suffer. Too many women have awakened from the race of their life to find themselves in divorce court.

As other things take precedence over your relationship, couple power is diluted. And then, all of a sudden, the "happy couple" finds themselves divorced. Oftentimes what has been beneath the glossy veneer of their relationship that other people see are hurting people who have failed to prioritize and have run themselves ragged. The woman has felt compelled to do it all, and the man has felt compelled to compete and conquer. Yet when it comes right down to it, they both miss what is most important—their relationship!

Sadly, marriage does not have a very high ranking in our society. It's easier to step out when the going gets rough. How often do you see celebrities switching spouses or boyfriends/girlfriends, going from relationship to relationship in search of fulfillment? One look at the tabloids says it all.

But don't let yourself fall into the grass-is-greener-on-the-other-side trap. When you get to the other side, you still have to mow it!

The reality is that marriage is like constructing a building. The foundation better be laid properly and square. The right material better be used, including rebar to make it tough and durable. Otherwise, the building that looks so good on the outside will develop fine cracks. Over time those cracks will widen across the entire surface, and the building will begin to disintegrate.

Dan, 40, met Lynn, 32, at an evening class at the local community college. Lynn was divorced and had a 13-year-old son. Dan had never been married and really enjoyed children. As the two got to know each other, they frequently included Joey on their dates. Dan thought, *Wow, this is the best of all worlds. If I ask her to marry me and she says yes, I get to be an instant father, too. This is what I've always wanted.*

Dan and Lynn were married three months later. When a friend advised them to wait and get some marriage counseling first, both declined. They were old enough to know what they wanted.

But once they were married, Lynn's attention turned immediately to her son, excluding Dan. She insisted that she had to be a mother first, and that Joey needed Dan's love. However, she wouldn't allow Dan to discipline Joey. "Joey's already been hurt enough by his father," she claimed. "He just needs your love."

Five years later, when Joey headed for college, Dan and Lynn's marriage fell apart. Instead of growing together, they had grown apart because the home had one focus—Joey. Now that Joey was in college, what was there to talk about? The foundation of their love had been hastily built, with no rebar, and the years of "child first" had developed cracks throughout their marriage. When Joey left, the building fell completely apart.

> All a husband really wants is to be pitied a little, praised a little, and appreciated a little.
>
> —Oliver Goldsmith

IS HE STARVING FOR YOUR ATTENTION?

Because of their top needs, most men have a lot of acquaintances and business contacts but very few meaningful relationships. That's why his relationship with you rates so high on his scale, *whether he'll tell you that or not.*

Do you realize what he gave up for you? He could be rebuilding cars with his buddies at the local gas station. Or hanging out at the restaurant with all the post-adolescents and college students for the summer. He could be having great conversations with his buddies, such as

"What do you want to do tonight?"

"Uh, I don't know."

What did I do before I got married? I grew up in a little town where the guys would hang out at the glorified hot dog stand. It had a huge parking lot. We guys would sit on the benches for hours on end, not doing much of anything. Some guys would work on their cars.

Guys who live by themselves eat the same meal seven days in a row. We wear the same clothes. We think nothing of eating bread with a little mold on it. We drink out of orange juice containers. Our apartments are decorated with a pyramid of pizza boxes, stacked in the corner—one for each day, Tuesday through Friday.

The point is, what we guys gave up for you wasn't much. Your guy certainly has a more interesting life with you! Did you know that?

But a woman can be so busy juggling home, career, and myriad relationships (something women are very good at) that often the person most left in the lurch is the one closest to her . . . her husband. Then add children to the mix, and there truly is little room for the first love of your life.

THE ONLY ONE HE TRULY WANTS TO BE INTIMATE WITH IS YOU. THAT'S HOW MUCH YOU MATTER.

Meanwhile, your husband is *starving* for your attention. He desperately needs time alone with you. Instead of looking at this with an "Oh, brother. Why does he have to be such a baby?" look at the flip side. What a compliment! The only one he truly wants to be intimate with is *you*. That's how much you matter. That's why it's so important to him to know he's number one in your life and not just another thing to check off your list.

He craves those romantic dinners out . . . as much as you need them. He needs time alone in the bedroom when the cell phone is turned off and your kids are at Grandma's for the night.

GOT A GAP?

Each of us has two selves: an ideal self and a real self.

The ideal self is how you would like others to see you.

The real self is who you really are.

The greater the gap between the ideal and the real, the more dissonance there will be in your life. If you try to be what you're not, you'll get yourself in trouble. You'll be continually disappointed with yourself and with others.

> Marriage is a two-way street, but sometimes you're the one who has to plow it.
>
> —Unknown

For example, if you are keen on others thinking that you have your life totally put together, that your house is always in pristine condition, and that you have the perfect family members (a husband, 2.5 kids, and a dog), you might be upset, to put it mildly, if you arrived home from work and found the kitchen trashed and your husband lounging on the sofa in his checked flannel shirt and sweats, eating leftover pizza, and watching a rerun of *Orange County Choppers*. Especially if your boss and his wife are coming over for dinner in an hour, and he'd promised he would start dinner for you.

Your ideal self had it all planned out. Your boss and his wife would arrive to a lovely, jasmine-scented home. Relaxed and happy, you'd welcome them at the door. You would be dressed in feminine evening attire, the dining-room table would be set with gold placemats accented with purple flowers, and you'd have the hors d'oeuvres arranged artistically on the coffee table in front of the sofa. You'd introduce them to your husband, who would be charm itself, and casually mention that a neighbor had asked to take your children to a play at a local community college. Your husband would have given Freda, the dog, a bath, so she would be at her fluffiest, friendly best to greet them with a tail wag before she exited the side door to play in the yard.

Later you heard secondhand what your guests really thought of their evening in your home. "She was so stressed. I could see it in her jaw," the wife said. "I wish people wouldn't invite us over if it's going to be stressful for them. Her living room smelled like leftover pizza. Makes you kinda wonder where she catered the dinner from, even if she made a big deal about its being homemade. You could tell her husband would rather be anywhere than home, that's for sure. His gaze kept wandering to the TV until he finally said he had to take the dog for a walk."

Trying to be who you are not is an awful lot of pressure for anyone! It's exhausting, and others see right through it—especially your husband. As the two of you develop emotional intimacy, he gets to know the real you and the things that you struggle with. The irony is that, because you struggle, sometimes you even try to hide the "real you" from the man who loves you most! It's like trying to hide who you really are from God. That doesn't work either.

THE COUPLES WHO SURVIVE AND THRIVE ARE THOSE WHO BRIDGE THE GAP BETWEEN THE IDEAL AND THE REAL IN THEIR LIVES.

The couples who survive and thrive are those who bridge the gap between the ideal and the real. They decide together what the next move in their marriage is. They spend some time looking backward at what "was" in each of their lives so they can move forward *together*. They don't care much about what others think. They care only what God and each other think.

For that, in the long run, is what matters most.

QUIZ

Do you know this woman?

Do you ever find yourself

    A. saying yes when you mean no, no, *No*!?

    B. laughing at a joke you don't understand so no one will feel bad (and you don't look humor deprived)?

    C. vowing never to chair the women's bazaar again? (The problem is you've said that for six years running.)

    D. smiling and complimenting your mother-in-law on her cooking when you absolutely loathe it?

    E. refusing to send your salmon back to a restaurant's kitchen when it arrives on your plate and it's still swimming?

For answers, see page 180.

Do you know this man?

    A. He's always right.

    B. He speaks about women with anger and disrespect.

    C. When he's wrong, it's someone else's fault.

    D. When things don't go his way, he throws an adult temper tantrum or withdraws into icy silence.

    E. After an argument, he equates making love with making up.

    F. He has to win in everything—business, ping-pong, and in love.

    G. He often complains that his employers or supervisors don't know what they're doing.

    H. He's skillful at making you feel guilty, even though you know you were right and you're doing the right thing.

For answers, see pages 180–181.

ARE YOU A PLEASER?

The trouble with women is that so many of you are pleasers.[1] You want to make sure everyone is happy, and you try so hard to make that work. But in the process, you end up assuming fault for things and situations and people that you have no control of. It's like the flight attendant who takes a lot of garbage in the form of rudeness and insults from a male passenger and the attendant says, "Thank you" to the man.

It's a continual juggling act to try to keep people happy. And it's not a healthy one. When women, who tend to be pleaser types anyway, come from dysfunctional family backgrounds, it is even more difficult. The pleaser is always "shoulding" herself. *What's wrong with me? I should have finished that project on time,* or *I should have picked up the kids. If I had, Mark wouldn't feel so stressed and unhappy. Then he wouldn't have yelled. It's all my fault. I'm so stupid.*

So many women run from thing to thing and try to accomplish everything at once because of that little voice inside that says, *You should have done something better.* That same voice takes away the sweetness of the victory you feel after accomplishing something wonderful. You're always thinking, even when someone says, "Great job," *Would you love me even if I didn't do that?* And because of that, you have a hard time saying no. So you ramp up the speed of life on yourself.

Meanwhile, the man who needs time with you gets shafted. Because you're so relationally oriented and are continually spending time with others, he always comes last. He won't say what he thinks, but what he's thinking is, *I guess I'm not very important to her anymore.*

Just because we live in a world where women can do and be anything they want—including surgeons, attorneys, and pilots—does that mean that *you* should do everything? Does it mean every opportunity you are given is a good one, and one that you should take right now?

Let me ask you a question: If your husband were sitting in my counseling room, would he say to me, "If I'm lucky, I get squeezed in between the late news and *David Letterman*"?

If you found out you had stage 4 ovarian cancer, what would you do differently in your life? Such a question separates the little details and "just busyness" from what really matters, doesn't it? Think about it.

A good marriage and family life are worth sacrificing for. To preserve time for marital intimacy (something we'll talk about more in the next chapter), not to mention being available for children, you may have to do without a few things. You may have to drive a car for ten years or more. You may have to forgo expensive vacations. You make have to make do with hand-me-downs or shopping in thrift stores rather than going to Nordstrom for the kids' back-to-school clothes.

But the sacrifices will be worth it. You are worth it. Your husband is worth it. And your children—whether now or down the road—are worth it.

Your big, strong husband is *desperate* for you to need him.

And if you don't have a love affair with your husband, someone else will.

How will you take on that challenge?

"MANSPEAK"

WHEN YOUR MAN IS DESPERATE FOR YOU

1. Listen to what he's saying.
2. Watch for clues and body language for what he's *not* saying.
3. Don't disrespect him, even when he's not as good at specific tasks as you are.
4. Think, *Could I do his job? How would I feel if I tried . . . and failed? Or if someone came in and took over that task because they were afraid I wasn't doing a good enough job?*
5. Be physically assertive and affectionate. Don't put his needs on hold for long. He really does *need you.*

HOW HOME-CENTERED IS YOUR GUY?

If a man is home-centered, it's likely because the queen is keeping the king pretty happy. A man's place is in the home (even if it's not his castle!). Many years ago people often said a woman's place is in the home. Women took great offense, but I think men belong there every bit as much as women! A man may have many bosses outside the home, but inside the home, he has the opportunity to kindly provide authority and to receive his rightful respect. Every healthy man needs a good home.

My travels often require me to be away from home, but I'm very home-centered. I can't wait to get home, and when I'm away from home, I call so often that I sometimes drive Sande crazy. "Look, Leemie," she says, "you may be on the road, but I've got to get a little work done around here!" A dream day for me is to be at home, putzing around the house with nothing to do. I just love it there. I can't even imagine wanting to be anywhere else.

If I'm a guy who's centered on something outside the home, I'll have to leave home to get my batteries recharged. I'll come home only reluctantly, and when I am home, my mind will be somewhere else. I'll act like I resent being home, and I'll grow short with people who "bother" me while I'm at home. My wife and my kids will get just the scraps, not the prime cuts.

If I'm home-centered—in large part because at home I feel like I'm respected, needed, and fulfilled and I have a wife who is focused on pleasing me instead of others—I'll do anything that will strengthen the home because that's my most important world. I won't think twice about sacrificing prestige at the office to be home by dinner. I won't let a boss browbeat me into missing my son's ball games or get home too late to tuck the kids into bed. I'll make sure the house gets repaired, because a healthy home is important to me—more important than anything else except, perhaps, my faith.

Is your guy home-centered? Instead of blaming him, ask yourself these questions:

1. Are you making home an exciting place to be?
2. Does he feel respected, needed, and fulfilled as a man?

Remember, those are your guy's three basic needs. Yet in the fast pace of a woman's world, it's easy to forget the one closest to you.

TAKE ACTION!
- Tell your spouse specifically what you love and appreciate about him. If you have children, do it in front of them.
- Set aside one night a week for just the two of you. Write it on the calendar in ink, and don't let anything change your plans.
- Send him a flirty e-mail or tuck a note in his lunch or briefcase that tells him how important he is in your life.

WHAT YOU CAN DO FOR YOUR DESPERATE MAN
Women are much better at multitasking than us men. You can talk on the phone and simultaneously set the table for dinner, change the laundry, and add a couple items to tomorrow's to-do list for work. All in the time it would take a guy to say, "Uh, hello?" into the phone.

Just watching you puts us into an awestruck state and, frankly, sometimes makes us dizzy. Because your life includes so many details and relationships and you seem to be doing a wonderful job, we're intimidated by you. We feel a little lost, a little inept.

When it comes right down to it, we know that you are our richest blessing. Here's what we'd love to see you do for us and yourself, if you asked us.

Don't overbook yourself.

In today's busy world with lots of choices, it takes determination and willpower to not overbook yourself. Especially since you're so relational and are wired to juggle a lot of things at once. But when we want time alone with you, we *need* time alone with you.

If you can rearrange your schedule to spend time with a girlfriend, we'd love the same consideration. It would be music to our ears to hear you say, "Honey, I was thinking about my schedule. It feels too packed, and I'm considering what I could do differently. Would you tell me what you'd like to see me eliminate? I want to be more available to you."

As you read that last paragraph, some of you bristled. *What do you mean? Make myself available? Who died and left you the boss? Are you from Neanderthalville? Where are you coming from, man?*

Stop right there. Comb, blow-dry, and fluff your bristles. Take a look around you and tell me what you see. Tell me what's happening to the relationships of people you work with. Tell me what's happening in your neighborhood. How many people do you know who are going through the tragedy of divorce right now? The pop psychologists of today are telling people, "It's all about you" and "Don't forget to renew your subscription to *Self* magazine." I'd like to remind you that the average marriage lasts seven years. What's going to make you different?

Maybe some of the key concepts in this book are worth your second thought. If you felt yourself bristling, perhaps you've been programmed or brainwashed into this almost paranoid view of men and their attentions in relationships: "Men! They're all alike!"

Then there are books such as *The Proper Care and Feeding of Husbands* by Dr. Laura that encourage a woman to put her husband first. The good news is that when you have a husband who understands the whole idea of mutual submission, it makes putting him first much easier! Then you love being a woman, because your man is attentive.

What kind of things does your husband do for you that show he really cares? What kinds of things can you do for him that show you really care?

Sande's mom died several years ago. Her birthday was September 25. So on September 25 I bought Sande a simple little card. The only words on it were *I love you*. I simply added the words *this day and every day* and drew an arrow down to the *I love you*. I gave her little pink roses with it.

Why did I do that? Because I know the way my wife thinks, and I want to be attentive to her needs. I wanted her to know that I remembered the day her mom was born. If I hadn't, Sande probably wouldn't have said a word about the day. She would have kept the knowledge to herself.

But I know that it's the little tender things we men do in relationships that answer the unspoken questions a woman asks every day: "Do you really love me? Do you really care?" To Sande, the fact I remembered her mother's birthday answered her unspoken questions with a resounding yes!

Melinda's questions about her husband's love and care were answered when Jeff took time to do what she knew he didn't have time to do: change the sheets on every bed in the house and do all the laundry while she was out of town and he was on a crash deadline.

Thinking of your guy first may mean that some things in the house don't get done—like dusting—for a few years, but we men don't care much about that anyway. If you're a mom of a two-year-old and a four-month-old, we're rather you take a nap when the kids do, instead of clean the house.

You only have so many hours in a day. Consider what will matter most down the road.

YOU NEED TO BE THE CARETAKER OF YOUR OWN HEART AND YOUR MARRIAGE.

Why not take a look at your calendar or DayTimer right now? What's on your schedule for today? for tomorrow? What things do you enjoy? What things bring stress into your life and relationships? Why not block out an evening to sit down and figure out what's really important to you?

If *you* don't start crossing off events, I guarantee that no one else will. You need to be the caretaker of your own heart and your marriage. If you simplify your life, your guy will be most appreciative . . . and you'll get the kind of husband that you long for.

Get creative!

Your life is not the same as it was when you were single. When you got married, you agreed—at least in theory—that your husband would be your first priority. If you have children, you've added yet another layer of responsibilities. And it can all add up to a lot to do, especially if you work outside the home too.

If you say, "It doesn't matter what it takes. I'm still going to be at the top of my company in 15 years" or "I can still work as an assistant at church," you may be piling up too much for you to do. If you are, both you and your family are going to pay the price.

Why not get creative? Before Carmen and her husband adopted their baby, both traveled a lot for their respective companies. After little Emma came into their lives, Carmen still had to work full-time to pay off the adoption fees. But she worked out a creative option with her company. They were short on office space. She was great at what she did and could do nearly all of it from home. They worked out an arrangement where she was only in the office two hours a week for meetings.

"Sure, I lost my penthouse view," Carmen says and laughs. "My coworkers said I had the best office. They couldn't believe I'd let that go. But I got the best deal in the long run. Full-time work, insurance benefits, and the privilege of being home full-time with my daughter. It isn't likely I'll ever get that office back, but I don't care. My priorities have changed with Emma in our life. Advancement in my profession used to be the most important thing to me, but no longer."

With the computer age, it's easier for a woman to work at home. So why not try some creative options? Work one day less a week and use that day to run errands so you won't have to do them on nights and weekends, when the stores are busier.

My assistant, Debbie, used to work with me in an office. I had the entire third floor of a large three-story building on the main drag of Tucson. I even had 16-inch block letters spelling out my name on the building. You could see it from the road. But that's all gone now. I value my assistant so highly that as her needs changed, I changed along with her. When she shared with me how difficult it was to get her daughter to school since her husband also worked, I was happy to change the hours. Today Debbie works completely out of her own home. It's a wonderful working arrangement for both of us, because then I get to be at my home as much as possible too. I love being able to drive my youngest daughter, Lauren, back and forth from school on the days that I'm not traveling.

Put him first, above the kids.

Let's say I'm three states away and I call my wife. I only have five minutes in between meetings, but I really want to touch base with her. During our short conversation, I am interrupted at least five times by the kids. After a while, I get tired of it and say, "I'll see ya." I hang up the phone and don't reveal what was on my heart to tell her.

Allowing the kids to interrupt your time with your husband tells him that you believe others' needs are more important than his.

He longs for you to say to the kids, "Not now. I am talking to your father."

That would prove that what he has to say is important to you, and that both of you are united in your stance with the children. It also tells his little-boy heart, *I'm not just a bother and a thing to check off during the day. You do value me for who I am.*

Children are great dividers. They will compete against each other and your husband for your attention. They're like Avis, the No. 2 car-rental company, whose slogan is, We try harder.

So don't let the kids interrupt you if you're talking to your husband. Give them a stern look if you have to. Put them in their place (number two, next to Daddy). Model for them that when Dad and Mom are talking, that's important. What the kids have to say—other than, "Uh, the house is on fire!"—can wait.

> What every parent needs to model: it's us against them.
>
> —Josh Billings

There will come a day when your little nest will be empty. When you look at your husband, don't you want to have things to say to each other? Then don't put all of your eggs in the child's basket. We men understand that sometimes the kids have to come first—when they are very young or sick. But if they *always* come first, we guys will become heartsick.

Let him breathe, *then* enlist his help.

You ladies have complicated days. Seventy-two percent of you with kids under the age of 18 are in the work force. You're not only bringing home the bacon, you're frying it up . . . and juggling 1,200 other things at once. Is it any wonder that when your guy walks in the door, you see the greatest relief pitcher in all of baseball? And you are more than willing to let him take over . . . immediately.

"Oh, you're home! I'm so glad! Can you watch the kids while I finish dinner and make some phone calls?"

But most guys need time to decompress from work and don't take too kindly to such a suggestion. They need to take a shower and shake off the day first. However, after he's had his shower and comes back downstairs, if he still looks draggy, you might say, "Kids, I know you want to play with Daddy, but he needs some time to relax first."

IT'S AMAZING WHAT WE MEN WILL DO WHEN WE FEEL HONORED AND INCLUDED.

Guess what? Your guy will usually rise to the challenge because, in his mind, you've honored him by putting him first. You've gone to bat for him and basically said, in a nice way, "Back off, kids. Daddy comes first, and he deserves a break." Ironically, that makes him feel ready to play. "Come on, kids, it's okay. I don't mind. Let's go out in the backyard and throw the baseball while Mom finishes dinner. Does that sound good? All right with you, honey?"

> The light of a man's heart is glimpsed through a woman's eyes.
>
> —Unknown

It's amazing what we men will do when we feel honored and included. Like the husband who took their three girls to the park on his day off and left his wife at home with time to herself. That day was her mental break—to drink tea, put her feet up, listen to music, and catch a few rays on the deck while she read a good book and took a nap.

You want to bet that when that man got home, he had a very happy wife. And because she was happy, she was also more willing to put the kids to bed early so they could have their very own celebration.

WHAT A MAN CAN DO TO MAKE HIS WIFE FEEL CHERISHED

1. Help with dinner, do the dishes, set the table. This is how women understand "I love you."
2. Clean up messes you didn't make . . . with no dramatic martyr expressions or sighs.
3. Chase frogs in the backyard with your kids to give her a break.

4. Realize that when you walk into your home after work, you belong to your family. So decompress *before* you get home, if possible.

5. Stand together with her on decisions. She doesn't want to feel like an island unto herself.

WHAT A WOMAN CAN DO TO MAKE HER HUSBAND FEEL HONORED

1. Put kids to bed when it's bedtime (early if your husband has that certain twinkle in his eyes . . .)

2. Allow yourself breaks during the day so you're not exhausted when he gets home.

3. Don't put him on hold or say, "Not now" when he's feeling amorous. Sometimes you need to throw your schedule out and fulfill that need. Other times, when it's impossible at that moment, you could say in a sexy tone, "You want to bet I want some of you too—*all* of you. Should we make it a date, then, at seven o'clock? I'll be ready for you . . . and thinking about you all day."

Sometimes we guys are thick in the head. Yet here's the good news: We're trainable! And we would do anything for your attention.

That's how much you matter.

#5 THING HE'LL NEVER TELL YOU

*"I've thought about sex 33 times today,
and it's not even noon."*

Guys are wired differently, and for a very good reason!

● ● ●

A 35-YEAR-OLD MAN sat in my counseling office. He looked deeply troubled.

"I can't help myself," he admitted. "I love to watch women walk down the street. The other day a hot brunette walked by. She turned me on . . ." He ducked his head. "You know what I mean, Doc. And I'm not even trying to look . . . really! I love my wife. What's wrong with me?"

You know what? There's absolutely *nothing* wrong with that guy!

Before you, as a wife, start to bristle, hear me out. What I'm going to reveal in this chapter is one of the most important things you need to know about your guy.

Do you know how many of the finest body parts that God ever created your husband has looked at today? If he drives an hour to work, he is bombarded with billboards selling everything from dog food to oil filters to cars. But they all share something in common—a smiling, sexy woman. Every place your husband goes, he is pounded with these images. He can't get his hair cut without being inundated by "come hither" women in the magazines. Madison Avenue uses flesh to sell just about anything.

And this creates a battle within your guy. A daily battle against adultery.

Like the time my buddy Moonhead and I went to the Buffalo Bills game, and a young woman in the aisle bent over. Her tail was eight inches from my face. I nudged Moonhead. "Hey, Moon, I just committed adultery." She stayed leaned over. And I tell Moonhead, "I just committed adultery again." We both looked at each other and laughed.

"Now just a minute, Dr. Leman!" you might be saying. "How could you be so callous about adultery? You're married, and you're looking at another woman's *bottom?* If I was your wife . . ."

Here's the point. Moonhead and I laughed because we both know it's a battle that we men face every day. Admitting it out loud helps us put it into perspective.

There's a big difference between men and women in how they are sexually wired. Let's say you and a girlfriend are shopping at the mall, and a handsome guy walks by. You and your girlfriend may exchange a grin and wiggle your eyebrows in appreciation, but that encounter is over. There has been no touch, no relationship—nothing personal to involve your emotions and life further. Most likely, you never think about that guy again. (Note that affairs occur with women when a man shows kindness, understanding for her needs, and touches her heart first. All these actions are usually in place before any sex occurs.)

But men, remember, are not relationally centered. They identify more with things. They are visually stimulated by looking. That means whatever your guy sees is imprinted on his mind. So if he sees a sexy woman in a red dress on the subway, he may see that same woman in his thoughts again later that night, a week later, even a month later.

And here's the kicker. He will be pounded with that image *even if he is happily married.*

DO THAT TO ME ONE MORE TIME. . . .

Men, on the average, have 33 sexual thoughts a day. When I told Sande that, she said, "That's sick."

You may be saying the same thing and thinking, *I only think about sex when he brings it up.*

Both men and women are designed for sex. Let me stop here, how-ever, to clarify a very important point. I believe wholeheartedly that

1. sex belongs in marriage.
2. sex belongs only in marriage—with one man and one woman committed for a lifetime.

That's the way God designed sex, and with good reason. The only "safe sex"—both emotionally and physically—is within the bounds of mar-riage. "Designer sex" is sex as the Creator intended it.

You may think I'm a relic of the bygone Victorian area, but I believe marriage is the only context in which a sexual relationship should take place. It is God's plan for one man and one woman to pledge their lives to each other, to encourage one another, to support one another, and to be totally loyal to each other in all areas of life, including sexuality, for as long as they live.

GOD CREATED SEX TO BE A POWERFUL EXPERIENCE THAT TRIGGERS EXTREMELY STRONG EMOTIONS.

God created sex to be a powerful experience that triggers extremely strong emotions. It was never meant to be an impersonal act. Like it or not, you become emotionally bonded to your sex partner. To those of you who have had sexual partners prior to your marriage, that explains why you have "flashbacks" of your previous sexual experiences and why you sometimes find it difficult to respond sexually to your husband.

Promiscuous sex is dangerous—physically, mentally, and emo-tionally. The research couldn't be clearer. A national study of over 1,800 married couples indicated that "the probability of getting a divorce was twice as high for couples who had cohabited prior to marriage compared to couples who had not. In addition, cohabitation prior to marriage related to lower levels of subsequent marital interaction and higher levels of marital disagreement and instability."[1]

That's why sex should be shared only with someone you love deeply, and if you love that person deeply enough to have sex with him or her, then you should love that person deeply enough to com-mit your life to him or her through marriage.

I love the little verse tucked away in the next-to-the-last book of the Bible. "Stay always within the boundaries where God's love can reach and bless you."[2] Sexual faithfulness is not just about keeping your hands out of some delightful cookie jar. It's about staying within the boundaries God has created for very good reasons. It's about enjoying a full and honest relationship in which God can bless you. And he can only bless you if the sexual act occurs within marriage.

WOMEN NEED A REASON FOR SEX. MEN ONLY NEED A PLACE.

It's been said that women need a reason for sex. Men only need a place. Men really need sex and are designed to need sex, to think about it, and to pursue it. A physically healthy married man cannot be fulfilled without it. Just think about this for a moment, ladies: If it were left solely up to you to pursue procreating the human race, there would be a lot fewer babies in the world!

Men are wired by God to enjoy the feminine form. It's normal for a man who loves his wife to walk by another beautiful woman in a red dress and think, *Wow, she's gorgeous.* Or for him to turn his head in a restaurant to follow a young woman in a red miniskirt.

The wife who thinks, *How could you? That's so dirty!* is missing the point.

The wife who thinks, *Hey, so he notices women in red? Mmm, what do I have in my wardrobe?* has grasped the point. Later, she will undoubtedly grab her husband's full attention by wearing that red little something she's got tucked in the back of her closet.

Statistics bear out what I'm going to say. What's going on in your sex life is a very good indicator of how the rest of your marriage is going. That's why I wrote a whole book entitled *Sheet Music: Uncovering the Secrets of Sexual Intimacy in Marriage* on this subject. It's well worth some nighttime reading, both for you and your spouse.

But let me state it for the record: Your husband can't get enough of you. Remember the old Captain and Tennille song, "Do that to me one more time. Once is never enough with a man like you." That's what your husband longs to hear you say. It's the language of his dreams, because it puts his needs first.

WHAT SEX DOES FOR A MAN

Sex is energizing for a man. It builds his confidence and boosts his overall sense of well-being. If he's in an unfulfilling job, he gets the strength to keep on doing what he's doing because he knows that there is a purpose for his work . . . and a willing wife waiting as a reward at the end of his long day.

Sex is the great equalizer in a man's life. If he meets with the accountant and is short on funds for his income tax or he got a bad job review, coming home to a willing wife makes it all better. It's amazing what things great sex can cure for men—everything from viruses, bacterial infections, impetigo, chicken pox, the flu, and, most importantly, any problem in marriage. For example, if he has a fight with his wife and later that day they have sex, all of his issues are gone. They've resolved themselves. The problem is that for the other half of the relationship—the female—the issues aren't resolved until they're talked about!

But turn your guy's sexual overtures down, and you'll be the recipient of some payback.

Let's say that you see your husband lounging on the couch when you have a million things to do. "Honey, can you take my mother grocery shopping?"

He barely looks up. "No, I can't."

"Why not? You're just watching the game."

"I'm busy."

"You don't look busy."

"I don't care what I look like. I'm busy. If your mom needs to go shopping, why don't you take her?"

What's going on here?

It's a delayed reaction. Admittedly, it's a cheap shot, but it happens all the time. The husband thinks to himself, *She turned me down yesterday for sex, so I'll turn her down now.*

Think of it this way. In a democratic society, if you have the right to put me down, what right do I have? Isn't it the right to put you down too?

HE SAYS: "ARE THE KIDS GOING TO BE HOME TONIGHT?"

He means: I want to romp and stomp and roll in the hay with you with no interruptions.

Admittedly we men do act like little boys sometimes. I'm not saying that's good or admirable, but that's the way we are. You're married to a real man. On the flip side, we are married to a real woman. And your man *craves* sex.

One of the most loving and holy things you can do in marriage is to pursue your husband sexually. If you do, you're helping him do part of his work. You see, men get a great deal of satisfaction from taking care of their families. And one of the items on your husband's job description is to be your lover.

Want a guy who comes around, stays around, and is your soul partner? A husband who goes to sleep with a smile on his face, thinking, *I've got to be the happiest guy in the world!?*

Then learn to be an extravagant lover. It will set your marriage and his satisfaction in cement.

QUIZ

What do researchers tell us about when men prefer to have sex?

    A. Any day, any time

    B. At the beginning of the day

    C. At the end of the day

    D. All day

For answers, see page 181.

What do researchers tell us about when women prefer to have sex?

    A. Any day, any time

    B. Early morning, before hair and makeup are done or could be messed up

    C. After a romantic dinner

    D. After the kids are tucked in bed

    E. When the kids aren't home

For answers, see page 181.

DO YOU LOVE YOUR BODY?

When I mentioned earlier in this chapter that you could don a little red number of your own to seduce your husband, I'll bet anything that you might have thought, *Yeah, right. I certainly don't have the figure of the woman in that red dress who walked by and turned his head.*

Guess what, ladies? Your husband wants you to take care of yourself, but those few extra pounds on the hips and thighs and having small breasts don't matter to your man. What he wants is a willing woman in bed. Being a willing wife will take pounds off your figure (or add them in the right places!) and make you look even more attractive to your husband.

BEING A WILLING WIFE WILL TAKE POUNDS OFF YOUR FIGURE (OR ADD THEM IN THE RIGHT PLACES!) AND MAKE YOU LOOK EVEN MORE ATTRACTIVE TO YOUR HUSBAND.

Just looking at you is an incredible turn-on for your man. In his eyes, you measure up—and you measure up quite nicely. So don't rob your husband of the pleasure of looking at you!

If it bothers you to look "too naked" (although there's humor in that phrase itself. Either you're naked or you're not!), why not dim the lights if that will help you? But don't dim them so much that he can't enjoy seeing your form.

Why is it so difficult for a woman to reveal her body, and especially in front of the man she loves most?

A woman's positive body image doesn't come easily—at least not to most of the women I've talked to. According to a *Psychology Today* survey, more than half of all American women dislike their overall appearance.[3] From my practice, I suspect it's *way* over half. Even women who know it's "politically correct" to accept their body type, still, in private, have a tendency to look in the mirror and wince.

Why is this? Everywhere you go, you see women who don't resemble you. You watch a sitcom and the moms on that show invariably

> Would you let someone else criticize you the way you criticize yourself?
> —Thomas Cash, *The Body Image Workbook*

wear tight sweaters with a touch of cleavage showing. You look down at your own size 30AA breasts and then at your expanding thighs and think, *Why can't I take five pounds from there and put it here?*

Or maybe you've developed some love handles and are afraid putting on some sexy lingerie would make your husband laugh instead of getting turned on. Perhaps you've given birth to three kids and have the stretch marks and pounds to show for it. So, even though your husband says your body still turns him on, you're reticent to "reveal all" to him.

Here's the irony. You are assuming that your husband won't be turned on by your body because you don't look like the models in the magazines. But guess what? Your guy doesn't look like the men in the magazines either! All those photos of models have been touched up anyway! That makes them not "real" people! But your guy is, and he's waiting to love you.

All of you.

HOW YOUR DADDY AFFECTS YOUR VIEW OF SEX

For those of you who grew up in a very strict, traditional home and were taught stringently about which body parts were off limits, it's hard to throw the switch on your wedding night. You may have been taught that sex is something best never spoken of. Your view of it may have become "Yes, sex is necessary to populate the world, but let's pretend that it doesn't even exist the rest of the time!"

Let me ask you: Were your parents affectionate? Did you have the kind of mom who always slapped her husband's hands away when he tried to flirt with her? Was your dad uncommonly cold toward you and your mom? Did he use his hand only to hurt and never to caress? Most importantly, how has this style of parenting influenced your view of sex with your husband?

Or maybe you saw the pornography in your dad's bedroom. The pictures imprinted themselves on your mind. And so did your dad's behavior toward you, when he would abuse you sexually. The use of pornography and sexual abuse often go hand-in-hand. You're so turned off by sex that you say, "I'm never going to do anything like that." If you have been sexually abused, it is all but impossible for you to trust another man. Every touch feels like a violation, even though you know your husband loves you. You are paralyzed by hurt and shame. And both you and your husband end up paying for it (whether he knows about it or not).

Ironically, the reason an abused woman runs to marriage is to avoid sex. If her husband is a nice guy, she knows he won't use and abuse her, so she figures that once she's married, she can kiss sex good-bye and never have to worry about it again.

If this is you, and you have abuse in your past, I recommend that you read Dr. Dan Allender's *The Wounded Heart,* which I think is the best book in the market on this subject. Another book every woman needs to read is *Intimate Issues: Conversations Woman to Woman* by Linda Dillow and Lorraine Pintus.

If you have a healthy relationship with your father, you will be more trusting of your husband and will have fewer inhibitions in bed. Fully giving yourself to your husband will feel natural and safe.

Even if you have added a few pounds and gravity has changed your hourglass figure.

THE GIFT OF SEX

God created sex

1. that you might create life.
2. for intimate oneness.
3. for knowledge.
4. for pleasure.
5. as a defense against temptation.
6. for comfort.

Wherever you are today, be assured that God is a God who redeems. He longs to show you that his gift can be erotic, fulfilling, free, and beautiful. But in order for you to enjoy the sexual relationship within your marriage, you have to throw out the mental tapes which play any message that conflicts with God's voice. You need to hear his voice alone. . . . And if you ask, he will redeem his beautiful gift in your life and make all things new.

—Linda Dillow and Lorraine Pintus*

*Adapted from *Intimate Issues,* by Linda Dillow & Lorraine Pintus (Colorado Springs, CO: WaterBrook Press), 6–10.

HOW LONG DOES IT TAKE?

Have you ever been putting on your mascara when your husband came up behind you and cupped your breast? Have you ever slapped his hand away with a curt, "Not now!"

Why *not* now?

How long does it take to caress a breast? Ten seconds? Twenty seconds? Can you really not give your husband that amount of time?

I know what you're thinking: *You don't understand, Dr. Leman. If I let him touch my breast, I'll be on my back looking up at the ceiling in 10 seconds flat. My clothes will be thrown all over the floor, my hair will get messed up, and I'll have to redo my makeup. Then I'll be late for work.*

Have you ever considered that being late to work once or twice a year could be just what your marriage needs?

But many times your husband just wants a quick feel. So next time surprise him by turning around and getting a quick feel of your own.

There's a huge difference between a wife who slaps a man's hands away and one who giggles mischievously, even engaging in one or two minutes of light petting, only to whisper in his ear, "This feels so delicious, but unfortunately, I really do have to get ready for work. Let's save it for tonight, when you'll get all you want and more." The second woman will have fulfilled her husband, even while staying clothed and keeping her hair in place. The first wife will have deflated her husband and eroded his masculinity, all for the sake of 60 to 90 seconds.

That's a costly minute.

TOP 10 WAYS TO KNOW WHEN THE HONEYMOON'S OVER

#10 A quickie before dinner is a drink.

#9 You sit next to the fire to keep warm.

#8 He's worn the same underwear three days in a row and the same shirt four days.

#7 Your head hits the pillow and you say, "Sex." His head hits the pillow and he says, "Sex." Now that you've had sex, you go to sleep.

#6 The average duration of a kiss is 1/10 of a second or less.

#5 The last flower you saw in person was at your uncle's funeral.

#4 You watched him read the entire sports page at breakfast.

#3 He notices you cut and colored your hair 16 weeks later.

#2 You now sleep the entire night.

#1 He no longer dances for you when he gets out of the shower.

WHY NOT NOW?

I have a bulletin for you: "Men have feelings too!" They're more fragile than most women realize. They want to please you, and their feelings get hurt far more easily than many women will ever know.

Do you want to give your husband a special treat? The next time he comes behind you and gently takes a breast in his hand, expecting you to slap him away, let him keep it there for a few seconds. When he finally pulls away, call out after him, "Hey!" in a forceful voice.

MEN HAVE FEELINGS TOO!

When you've got his attention, say, "You forgot the other one."

Or better yet, move his hand to another favorite spot.

It will be a conversation your husband will never forget.

You see, men *do* think differently. When I see Sande bending over to unload the dishwasher, I'll say something like, "Do you want to know what I'm thinking right now?"

"No, Leemie," she'll say, "I *don't* want to know what you're thinking. Go find something to do."

The mere sight of a woman bending over (flash back to my anecdote about the woman at the Buffalo Bills game) does something profound to a man. We're visual creatures, and we're given visual clues all day long. Combined with the testosterone coursing through our bodies, that makes many of us live in a heightened state of sexual alert.

Here's another scenario. If I say the same thing to Sande when she's bending over the dishwasher, she might say, "Leemie, Mr. Happy has this habit of getting himself all excited at times where there's not a chance he's going to get lucky. But I'll tell you what: Mr. Happy is going to get quite a workout tonight. I'm looking forward to it. In fact, there's nothing I'm looking forward to more."

When Sande does this, it's even better than her immediately giving in! You know why? She's using the power of anticipation. And for a man, emotionally, anticipation is even better than participation.

Does that surprise you? Think about it. How long does participation last? Ten minutes for a quickie? Twenty minutes on average? Forty-five to 60 minutes if you really take your time?

But a wife who tells her husband, "Tonight's the night!" is giving her husband an *entire day* of pleasure. Twenty minutes will hardly go by without your husband thinking of you, imagining you, wanting you. Doesn't that sound wonderful? To have your husband thinking loving and affectionate thoughts about you all day long?

The words and actions you choose are really important. When your husband is about to leave the house and he comes to give you a perfunctory kiss, surprise him by giving him a real kiss—practically cleaning his bicuspids in the process. Then say, "I've got plans for you later, buddy, so hurry home from work." If you do, you're going to be on his mind all day long.

I remember after a few years of marriage, Sande said to me, "It sure doesn't take much to get you going, Leman." The inexperienced woman may think, *What have I gotten myself into?* I talk to young wives all the time who are truly shocked at the frequency and duration of their husband's sexual interest. Some have told me that they thought if they just gave in and had sex five days in a row, their husband would be "cured." Not a chance. He might be smiling this week, but next week, he's still going to be interested.

This "always on" mentality men have isn't a conspiracy; it's how God made us. Keep reminding yourself of that. God himself thought it was important that your husband be chemically drawn to you and motivated to get physically close to you on a regular and consistent basis.

How does a woman measure love? How does she know she's truly cared for? It's usually not in the bedroom. It's usually in the day-by-day little things that matter to her. It's the lifestyle of affection that she wants.

If you want that lifestyle of affection, fulfill your man sexually. Then, instead of resenting requests to stop by the store or look at a leaky faucet, he'll jump with eagerness to meet your needs. Instead of being cold and distant when you talk to him, he's going to want to hear what you have to say.

"But, Dr. Leman," you might say, "I tried that, and it didn't work."

YOU CAN'T JUST "TRY" SEX IN MARRIAGE; IT HAS TO BECOME A WAY OF LIFE.

You can't just "try" sex in marriage; it has to become a way of life. One good time of sex will make a man thankful . . . for a while. But if you turn him down the next five times when he approaches you, he'll think about the five rejections, not that one special night. Because of a man's chemical makeup, sex feels like a need to him. When a woman uses that need to manipulate her guy, he will become resentful. But when she graciously and eagerly meets that need, he becomes very thankful. And he shows that in all areas of his life with his wife.

The sexually fulfilled man is the kind who drives to work thinking, *I must be the happiest man alive. I'm so glad I married that woman!* He's the same man who drives home thinking, *What special thing can I do for my wife this evening?* And you know what? Even if he has a bad day at work, he will still be thinking that because he knows what he's going home to.

Giving and receiving spontaneous sexual gestures can work wonders for your marriage. So why *not* now, and why *not* here?

WHEN THE ROLES ARE REVERSED

In 15 percent of marriages, the roles are reversed. Instead of the wife who has the proverbial headache when the husband wants sex, it's the man who has the headache. He says he's too tired, too exhausted, and/or has too much on his mind. Why does this happen?

In most of these situations, it's because of the view the man was brought up with regarding sex. He was taught that sex was bad, naughty, or dirty, or he had a strong female in the home who slam-dunked him. In essence, he's being passive-aggressive to see if he can control you. He wants to hear you beg for sex. He may also be hiding from sex with you because of homosexual tendencies. He may have been sexually abused himself, or had a buddy or a father who introduced him to pornography.

If this is happening in your marriage, please ask your husband to get some counseling. Go with him, if he is comfortable with that.

Did you know that four out of ten girls have been abused? I really don't know how many men, but my guess would be one in ten.

I want to be clear here. You or your husband may have been sexually abused, but that does not give you the right to wallow in your issues. My question to you is this: what are you going to do about it? Yes, that may have happened in your past, and your relationship(s) have paid a price. Now is your time to take control, to bring more health into your life and relationships. Will you be gutsy enough to do it?

A man who lived with a domineering and controlling mother may dislike a sexually aggressive wife and "play tired or dead" when she wants sex. A man who found gentle love with his mom, and who was taught to respect her, generally won't have too much trouble becoming sexually intimate with his wife.

HE WANTS TO PLEASE YOU

Your husband wants to have sex with you for his own sexual relief. But even more than he wants his own pleasure, he wants to please you. He enjoys seeing how much you enjoy the pleasure he can give you. As he's watching you, he's thinking to himself, *I did that to her, thank you very much.*

If he fails to do that, he'll end up feeling inadequate, lonely, and unloved. After all, each man wants to be his wife's hero (more on that in chapter 7).

> YOUR GUY WANTS TO BE ROMANTIC, BUT HE MAY BE WORRIED THAT HE CAN'T PULL IT OFF.

Once again, the little boys we men once were, we still are. We still want to please the primary woman in our life. When we were six, that meant pleasing Mommy; when we're 26 or 36 or 46 or 66, it's our bride. That means your guy wants to be romantic, but he may be worried that he can't pull it off. That he won't know what to do or that he'll fail.

So if you're smart, and you understand how important competition and winning are to a man, you'll help him. You'll keep him intrigued and satisfied.

You can be married without having any sex at all. You can still talk over dinner, celebrate the holidays, and—if you adopt—raise children. You can buy each other anniversary gifts, share intimate conversations, and even, in an emergency, share toothbrushes or bring an urgently needed roll of toilet paper.

But something would be missing.

A good sex life colors your marriage from top to bottom. It takes the humdrum and boring out of all the daily things you do for each other.

Think about it: 90 percent of life is filled with mostly boring stuff, like changing dirty diapers, cleaning up countless spills, paying the

A GOOD SEX LIFE COLORS YOUR MARRIAGE FROM TOP TO BOTTOM.

bills, filling the gas tank. And many men and women often have to work in deadly dull jobs—checking food at the grocery store, pounding nails into a roof, or adding up the same batch of figures. I've even met accomplished lawyers and dentists who were bored out of their minds with their professions, but financial obligations insisted that they keep doing them.

Into this world of obligation and responsibility, God has dropped something absolutely fabulous into our laps. At the end of the day—and sometimes at the beginning—when our work is done and the kids are in bed and we're home from work, we can touch each other and kiss each other and pleasure each other in such a way that the world feels like it is light-years away. We're transported to another place and removed to another time, and it's a glorious feeling indeed.

HOW TO GROW YOUR OWN CRAVING FOR SEX

A fulfilling sex life is one of the most powerful marital glues a couple can have. But often the biggest enemies of sex among women are being too busy, tired, and stressed.[4]

One women's magazine puts it best:

> What's the first thing to go when you're busy, tired, and stressed? If you said sex, you're not alone. An estimated 24 million American women say they don't have time, are too exhausted, or just aren't in the mood for sex, and more than a third of *Redbook* readers say that being too tired is their number-one excuse for not having sex. So we put it off for later—but later can easily become never. In case you haven't noticed, abstinence doesn't make the loins grow hotter, it just begets more abstinence.
>
> Sex on the other hand, begets more sex. Studies show that lovemaking elevates the levels of brain chemicals associated

with desire. So the best way to increase your yearning for sex is to have it.[5]

Having a great sex life is an exhilarating experience; it can bond a husband and wife like cement until there is nothing that they won't do for each other.

But it all starts with taking a meat cleaver to your schedule. Do I sound like a broken record? I have been speaking and writing for years about how the overcommitted pace of American families is killing us socially, relationally, and psychologically. We are simply too busy. Many families I work with could easily cut out 50 percent of their activities and still be tired. That's *not* an exaggeration. Most families who see me are often shocked at the way I can take a meat cleaver to their schedule.

When we live at the pace of a NASCAR race, sex is one of the first things that goes. Once again, if you want to improve your sex life as a couple, you need to examine your relationship outside the bedroom. What are you doing that is keeping you from sexual intimacy?

WHAT ARE YOU DOING THAT IS KEEPING YOU FROM SEXUAL INTIMACY?

When *Redbook* magazine ran a poll on its Web site asking, "What would you do with an hour's worth of free time?" over 10,000 men and women responded. Eighty-five percent of men and 59 percent of women answered *sex*—wide majorities in both cases. Just 12 percent of women chose shopping or extra sleep, followed by watching TV, exercising, reading, and eating.[6]

What does this tell you? If you had extra time, the majority of you wouldn't head out to the mall. You wouldn't pick up a book or turn on the television or go to the gym. You'd get naked with your spouse—and your marriages would be much better for it.

"MANSPEAK"

WHY YOU WANT TO MAKE HUBBY HAPPY

1. A sexually fulfilled husband will feel good about himself.
2. A sexually fulfilled husband will take on his life work with an unmatched vigor and purpose.
3. A sexually fulfilled husband will do anything for you.
4. A sexually fulfilled husband appreciates the important things in life.

DID YOU KNOW THAT, TO YOUR GUY, your *attitude* toward sex is more important than your breast size, your waist size, your thigh size, or the length of your legs? The vast majority of men say they would rather have a wife who's a little on the plain side but has a sexually available attitude than a drop-dead gorgeous woman who freezes her husband out.

HOW WILLING ARE YOU?

A positive attitude also means appreciating your husband. It means respecting, needing, and fulfilling him.

If you deny him, resent him, or cut him down for what he is designed to need, you emasculate him. But if you fulfill his need for sex with great willingness in both words and attitude, you'll make him feel like the luckiest man on the planet!

That's a lot of power! But our Creator must have felt you could handle this power since he designed men and women this way. If God were to measure your kindness and generosity solely by how well you treat your husband in this area, what do you think he would say?

Following are a few ideas to make your man extra happy in this area.

Let him enjoy looking.

My wife always looks beautiful. When she gets up in the morning, she looks nice. But still she has to put apricot stuff all over her face to "revive it." One day, after her usual morning routine, she put on a white camisole, and then a white knit sweater that looked, to my guy's eyes, like white rope tied together very loosely. So I said to her, "I'd love see that—*just that*—on you sometime."

Just saying those words made me frisky . . . even though I know it would be so unlike my modest, firstborn wife to surprise me and do such a thing. But if she did? Oh, boy! I'd be one deliriously happy guy.

Your husband is designed to look—and to enjoy looking. What would he like to see on you?

Surprise him!

> It's the differences between male and female that make love and romance so exciting.
>
> —R.C. Sproul,
>
> *The Intimate Marriage*

Anne and Dave had been married for eight years. For the past two years, they had been working hard to establish their own business. The long hours were starting to pay off, but Anne knew the stress was wearing on Dave. It seemed like they had less and less time at home together.

So one day at lunchtime, she pulled him into his private office, locked the door, and shut the blinds. Right there in that office they had a sexual interlude. The rest of that day Dave was a happy, relaxed guy. In fact, he grinned every time he sat at his desk for the next week.

Dave felt like every man wants to feel: pursued and needed. There was no doubt in his mind that his wife enjoyed being with him. And he appreciated her imagination, too!

So don't be a "boring in bed" baby. Risk using your imagination, and you'll win your guy's heart!

The challenge, of course, is that surprising your husband takes time, energy, and foresight—something an overly busy woman simply doesn't have. But here's the irony: A man who is respected, needed, and fulfilled is the kind of man who, when his wife calls and asks him to pick up a gallon of milk at the grocery store on his way home, even though he passed that store three miles ago—will go back and get that milk.

If your guy feels loved and prized and surprised by your passion for him, he'll knock down walls for you.

> If you don't have to take a shower afterwards, you haven't had great sex.
>
> —My buddy Moonhead

Make sex an all-day affair.

Some of the best sex lasts all day, even though both partners may spend the first ten hours of that day ten miles apart. I talked a lot about this in my book *Sex Begins in the Kitchen.*

Imagine what a man would feel like if he woke up, stumbled into the bathroom, and turned on the light, only to be startled by some vivid writing in red lipstick at the corner of the mirror:

> *Good morning, Mr. Sexy!*
> *Let's put the kids to bed early tonight.*
> *I've got some exciting plans!*
> *XOXOXO*

For a guy, anticipation is as good as participation in sex, so why not do something out of character for you? Tuck a piece of intimate clothing in his briefcase or lunch bag. Send him a tempting e-mail.

Sex is not a "single event." The preparation for it for both you and your husband is in the way you treat each other in the little things, all throughout the day.[7]

Don't make Mr. Happy live by a schedule.

To the chagrin of many a wife, Mr. Happy doesn't live by a schedule. In fact, Mr. Happy doesn't even know what a schedule is. He also has a very short memory.

For example, let's say you and your husband had a nice, long, and leisurely session of lovemaking the night before. The next morning your husband is watching you stretch to put a book in a bookcase. It's Saturday morning and you're just working around the house, so you didn't bother to put on a bra. As you stretch, your breasts move provocatively inside your T-shirt.

If you are a woman, you're probably thinking like a woman: *We had sex last night. I haven't showered yet. I'm wearing grubby clothes. The seduction factor has to be 1 on a scale of 1 to 10.* Yet you notice that within seconds your husband has come up to give you a hug from behind and you're suddenly aware that Mr. Happy is not exactly "resting." You think, *What's wrong here? We just did it last night!*

But in married sex, there is no scoreboard or contest. With men, *spontaneity* is the name of the game. Since men are driven by sight, a glance at a woman in her underwear or getting out of the shower can be enough of a trigger—especially if it has been a couple of days. That's all it takes.

Arouse his senses.

Let's say your husband hears the shower running at 10:30 p.m. Just the sound of the water makes him frisky. He's thinking, *Oh man, I could get lucky tonight.* When his wife walks out sporting a new nightie that conveniently displays her soft headlights, he's suddenly a little boy.

"Wow! Is that new?"

Now here's the smart wife. She looks him right in the eye, bends toward him to let her breasts work their magic, and says, "I got it just for you."

It's all about the presentation.

My wife, Sande, is a master of the artful presentation. She's always been great at presenting old stuff in a new way. She can turn an old lampshade into a work of art by re-covering it with the right fabric.

You can do the same thing by learning how to present yourself—to wrap yourself, to wrap your room, to wrap the moment in a seductive allure tailor-made for your husband. Maybe you want to emphasize your eyes, your legs, or something else. Learn to accept that as your strength, and shamelessly flaunt it to full effect in front of your spouse.

If your breasts are your strong point, buy lingerie that brings all the attention to your chest. If your best-selling point is your eyes, or maybe your mouth, wear makeup that will draw your husband's attention to those features. Use what you have to full effect, and don't worry about your less admirable features.

> A successful marriage requires falling in love many times, always with the same person.
>
> —Mignon McLaughlin

What your husband wants the most is for you to enjoy his body. To explore it. Revel in it. Play with it. Touch it. Exclaim over it.

Your body is a wonderful thing. It's one of the best gifts you can ever give to your husband. So don't fall into the "but I'm not as beautiful as the models in the swimsuit edition of *Sports Illustrated*" trap. If you are generous with your body, both you and your husband will enjoy the results!

And it's not sight only that will catch us.

When I was in charge of student orientation at the University of Arizona, five girls told me, "We walk by 2,000 guys on campus every day, but we're not meeting any guys."

"Do you have a popcorn popper?" I asked.

This surprised them. "Yeah, we do. But what—"

"Then here's what I want you to do," I said. "Pick any men's dorm you want, spread out a sheet, and plug in your popcorn popper. Pop some popcorn and spread the popcorn out all over the sheet. Then make several more batches to put into bowls and see what happens."

When those girls came back with their report, they were giddy. Not only had they pulled it off, but they had found a lot of male bears hibernating in the upper hallways. When the smell of popcorn drifted into those stairways, it wasn't long before the slumbering males, awake from their winter naps, were drawn toward the females sitting on the floor, surrounded by popcorn, in the corner of the dorm. To a guy, the smell of popcorn rivals any perfume you could wear.

The story continues. Then the guys they had met decided to pay a visit to the girls' dorm. They brought a popcorn popper and did the same thing. It became a tradition between these groups of students until they eventually paired off.

It all started because five women risked looking a little silly to initiate and surprise the men in that dorm. Not only did they meet the guys on their turf, but they played to the heightened senses of the men.

Did you know that a woman can make many men's heads turn simply by choosing the right perfume? Men can become puppy dogs, utterly conquered by certain aromas.

"Will you marry me?"

"I don't even know you!" you gasp.

"It doesn't matter—if you'll always smell this good, I want to be your husband."

Tell him what feels good.

The rule that men are simple and women are complex works in every facet of life, including sex. What feels good to a woman on Tuesday night won't feel as good on a Saturday night. Most men have the mentality, because of their get-the-job-done nature, "I'm going to figure this out and get it down pat. And then we'll do the same thing for years!" That's why men can go to a restaurant and eat the same thing for four years, while women, by their very nature, want to try something new and take a half hour to order off the menu they've seen zillions of times.

So why not help your husband be creative? Help him succeed in your lovemaking by telling him what feels good and what doesn't. He'll be glad for your feedback . . . and glad he didn't have to risk asking for it or playing the 20 Guesses and You're Out game.

Clear your schedule.

I'll say it again. In order to provide for this need in your man's life, you need to slow down.

How do couples begin to overcome the effects of weariness? If you truly want to make your family life and your sexual life more meaningful, you're going to have to give up a few things. No more running around five out of five weekday evenings. I'd say if you're gone more than two evenings a week, something needs to give. Why not cross things off your calendar?

If you make room for sex, your attitude will be more willing, your husband will be eternally grateful, and you'll both enjoy your marriage more.

#6

THING HE'LL NEVER TELL YOU

"I told you I didn't want to go!"

What your man fears more than anything else . . . and how you may
be doing that very thing in subtle ways.

● ● ●

IT WAS THE second time in six months that Jan had dragged her husband, Greg, to one of her community service banquets. He'd had
enough. It didn't matter that his wife was giving him "the eye" for not
being social. He spent most of the evening sitting glumly at a table
while everyone else chatted. And when he wasn't at the table, he was
dragging his feet toward the punch bowl to refill her glass.

"What is wrong with you?" she hissed at him later in the car. "You
acted like an idiot. And you embarrassed me in front of all my friends."

What was his response? "I *told* you I didn't want to go!"

The rest of the drive home was made in icy silence.

When Greg and I talked about that situation later, he admitted,
"I hate socializing. It makes me feel awkward, alone, and embarrassed. I
drive a UPS truck, get up as early as a dairy farmer, and work long hours.
I'd rather she go alone, and I'll stay home with the kids. I love the time
with the kids. Besides, we'd save money on the babysitting. But instead,
I have to spend the evening standing by the punch bowl looking and

feeling like an idiot (Note: I could relate! Remember my earlier story when I felt like that?) while my wife flits happily from person to person. Frankly, I don't even like the people she hangs out with. I don't understand the projects she does, so I have nothing to say about them. I keep telling her that I don't want to go to those events and that I'd rather stay home. But she won't take no for an answer. It drives me crazy!"

Let's get down to brass tacks. Because his wife didn't take Greg's no for a no, he felt majorly dissed or disrespected. His wife was saying, by her response, "Oh, but you don't really mean that. Of *course* you want to go with me."

But Greg didn't, and even when he said no, she pressed the issue so much that he sighed, gave up, and went to the event. He was beat verbally in the fight to go to the event—his wife could outtalk him any day. So he did the only thing he could. He acquiesced to go to the event, then gave her and everybody else the passive-aggressive treatment. While he was sitting quietly at the table, inside he was yelling, "*No, No, No!* I told you I didn't want to go, but you made me. You don't respect me or my wishes!"

WHAT DOES *HONORING* REALLY MEAN?

Honor, per *Webster's Dictionary*, means "to hold in high respect, to revere, to show a courteous regard for."

Part of honoring your husband means honoring his opinions and views. It means taking his no for a no, instead of trying to turn him into one of your girlfriends who would enjoy the event with you (as we talked about in chapter 3). But this is harder than it sounds to a woman because your world is defined by having your guy experience things *with* you. You can only be truly happy when the experience is shared with him. Not so for your guy.

Yet he finds himself getting dragged into social situations where he isn't comfortable, feels useless and stupid, and has to be, by default, the wallflower at the party. Like Timothy, who got dragged to a scrapbooking festival because his wife wanted him to see how much she loved that kind of thing. He spent an entire Saturday staring at "cute" die cuts and helping his wife with her shopping bags. He was bored to death. The only thing that kept him from going crazy was dreaming of motocross racing the following weekend.

Before you drag your husband into this kind of situation, *ask* him.

And then accept his response as the truth. Read his lips and his body language. Even if he's not verbally saying no, you should be able to read "I don't want to go" by the stiff, determined jaw or the frown. If an activity is not his cup of tea, don't force him to go. Would you like to change the oil on a car? overhaul a small-block Chevy V-8? mountain bike across the Rockies? or enjoy a monster-truck night at the fairgrounds? Some of you may, but many of you wouldn't. So then why do you drag your guy to scrapbook stores, floral conventions, antique shows, or a "how to remodel your kitchen space" workshop?

READ HIS LIPS AND HIS BODY LANGUAGE.

Why not let your guy be a guy? And be the guy he is? I know some guys who love to grow orchids and listen to opera, but they are still real men's men.

Let your guy stay home when you do things that only you like to do. Honor and respect your man by taking his no for a no, and his yes for a yes. Remember, men are straightforward and will tell you what they think. The problem comes when you try to manipulate those words to get him to do what you want him to do. *Oh, he doesn't really mean that,* you think. *Of course he wants to go. He just wants me to persuade him a little bit more. . . .*

No, actually he wants you to lay off. (Take it from a guy who knows.) He wants to stay home, put up his feet, belch, eat cold leftover pizza, and have some peace and quiet while you enjoy your social evening. In fact, if you gave him a choice of cleaning out the cat's litter box and going to the event with you, which one do you think he'd choose?

IF YOU GAVE HIM A CHOICE OF CLEANING OUT THE CAT'S LITTER BOX AND GOING TO THE EVENT WITH YOU, WHICH ONE DO YOU THINK HE'D CHOOSE?

Honoring your husband means "showing a courteous regard for" him in every area of life. If a girlfriend said, "I really don't want to go eat in that restaurant," would you force her to go there with you? Why not show your husband the same respect?

WHAT HAPPENS IN VEGAS, STAYS IN VEGAS

While we're on the subject of girlfriends, ladies, I wanted to share with you something very important to us men. We do not like to be discussed with your girlfriends. In fact, we detest it. Because we're so fragile underneath our bravado, we can't stand to be the subject of your lunch: "You know what he did?" you say to launch the discussion, then you shake your head with disgust and tell all.

"You've got to be kidding!" a girlfriend says and laughs. "Well, last week Mike . . ."

And you're off running with some wild tales of what we men do. They might be the truth, but we still don't like it. Would you like it if we said in front of a buddy, "My wife's getting really flabby in the thighs"?

Yes, we men do stupid things every once in a while (okay, maybe more than once in a while), but revealing them to the world embarrasses us and emasculates us. It would be like somebody pointing out your worst body feature and then going on and on about it. That's how it makes us feel.

Think about it this way. Whenever you talk to your girlfriend or your sister or your mother or your husband's mother about your man and the goofy thing he did, you are violating your marital vow to be faithful. And that's dangerous. So is lumping "all men" into the same category. We don't need you talking to anyone else about what is private and should stay between a husband and wife.

Because we guys are performance based, we don't need laughter about our performance in a certain area. We need mercy, grace, your understanding, and your belief in us.

Just as you need us to believe in you.

Yes, I know women love to "share" (I say this with a twist of my lips). We know it is natural for you to share experiences with your girlfriends. But you need to button your lips where your guy is concerned. If you do, you will earn and maintain your husband's trust in you.

There is an exception, however, to the girlfriend gab fest. If you want to share *good* gossip about us, go right ahead.

IF YOU WANT TO SHARE *GOOD* GOSSIP ABOUT US, GO RIGHT AHEAD.

When Monica miscarried her baby, she was emotionally and physically exhausted. Brian, her husband, is one of those guys who is kindness itself, but very much a "real guy." For the first three months after her miscarriage, he gave up his every-other-Saturday breakfast with two guys from his church so Monica could have breakfast with two girlfriends who happened to be the wives of those two guys. Brian stayed home and took care of their two-year-old, Michael, and spent that time cleaning the house. It may not have been the kind of clean that Monica would have done, but she was very grateful.

"I never would have made it without Brian's help," Monica told Sue and Keri over breakfast. "He's the greatest guy in the world. Boy, did I choose right! I know he didn't lose the baby from his body, but he's so understanding of how I feel. I'm so glad he's Michael's daddy. And I hope someday we have another baby, so that baby can have Brian for a daddy too."

Guess what? Two weeks later, Brian ran into Craig, Keri's husband, in Ace Hardware. "You should hear those girls talk," Craig said, laughing. "I think you just won the Husband of the Year award, from what they say." He filled Brian in on what the wives had talked about.

How do you think that made Brian feel? Especially in front of another guy? Like a million bucks!

Good gossip gets around, and it can do amazing things to a man's chest, like make him puff with the good kind of pride inside. It can also do amazing things to his willingness to do things like help around the house.

Although Brian and Monica had agreed only on her going out to breakfast every Saturday for the first three months, it became a tradition in their home. Every-other Saturday, Brian went out with the guys. The in-between Saturdays, Monica went out with the girls. And whoever stayed home watched Michael and cleaned the house. For the past 16 years now, the three women have had two Saturday breakfasts a month, and the three men have had two Saturday breakfasts a month. Last week they all got together to celebrate (and mourn) Michael going off to college!

So if you're going to share some gossip of your own, why not share some good gossip?

DOWN WITH THE PUT-DOWN

When I used to coach football for kids from the barrio, I learned a hard lesson. I once showed the quarterback, a 15-year-old boy, how to set his feet when he took the ball from the center.

He threw the ball at me and yelled, "Then you do it!" and stomped off.

What was going on there? He left because he was embarrassed. In Hispanic culture, you don't call a guy down in front of his buddies.

The same is true for all men. So often, without knowing it, a woman can cut down her guy in front of others.

"I asked you to take the garbage out, and it's still sitting here."

"Why didn't you clean out the garage? That's your job!"

"You didn't bring your paycheck home again?"

These statements may seem like fact to you, but if you say them in front of his buddies, you will make your husband angry. Nobody likes to be embarrassed in front of his friends. Would you like it if your man said in front of your girlfriends, "Your hips are looking a bit wide these days. Shouldn't you go on a diet?"

Wouldn't you be embarrassed . . . and downright mad?

> A good marriage is one in which there are more put-up-withs than put-downs.
>
> —Unknown

Never forget that rule of a democratic society: If you have the right to put me down, I have the right to put you down. And believe me, ladies, we men can win at the put-down.

So if you have something to say (as mad as you might be), wait until you and your husband are *alone*. Then, being careful of your tone of voice, address the subject fairly and straightforwardly. Don't point a finger.

Remember the story in chapter 1, where I embarrassed my daughter by what I wore to school? Sande took a big risk telling me the truth that day. I might have gotten mad at her. But because she values honest, open communication and commitment to family is at her core (note: two of the top three needs of women were at play in our communication), she took the straight route to letting me know about the situation.

She could have harangued me: "Kevin Leman, how could you be so stupid to wear bedroom slippers to our daughter's school? Don't you know how much you embarrassed her—and me? The next time you go out the door, I'm going to have to check your outfit. If you *ever* do that again, I'll . . ."

Instead she told me the truth and nothing but the truth—that it was important to my daughter I never show up that way again.

Respecting your guy doesn't mean letting him get away with murder (or, in my case, nasty-looking slippers). It doesn't mean sighing melodramatically and saying, "Well, boys will be boys."

It means speaking the truth in love.[1]

No dissing.

No you-should-haves or you-oughtas.

THINGS THAT WILL MAKE YOUR GUY REALLY ANGRY
1. Put him down in front of his friends.
2. Talk about your relationship to others.
3. Let him hear about something important third hand.

"I CAN'T FIX THE TOILET!"

Because we are born competitive and with a need to conquer and win, we men don't want to admit that we can't do something that a guy should know how to do.

So when you say to us, "Oh, honey, the toilet keeps running and running. I think it's broken again," the first thing we want to do is *try* to fix the toilet. We're on a mission to conquer that toilet, and we're determined to win! So off we head to Home Depot or Lowes, where we spend several hours talking to the guys there (while you, meanwhile, are having to run outside to use the bushes in the backyard because you're afraid the toilet will overflow if you flush it). We get schematics about toilets—even if we can't read them. We come home armed with a whole arsenal of fix-it stuff and enough confidence to slay the toilet dragon.

WE COME HOME ARMED WITH A WHOLE ARSENAL OF FIX-IT STUFF AND ENOUGH CONFIDENCE TO SLAY THE TOILET DRAGON.

Then we arrive home to find out you've already called the repairman, and he's at the house right now, doing the job that we intended to do.

How do you think that makes your guy feel? Bummed. Like he's a failure. *So she thought I couldn't do it,* he thinks. *She didn't even wait long enough to let me try.*

Karen had waited nearly six weeks for her husband to replace a broken window. And that was after she'd already waited six weeks to get the window after the four weeks it had taken Barry to get around to ordering it. Her patience was just about used up.

That day she was talking with her neighbor Olivia about her frustration with the window when Olivia's husband pulled up in the driveway.

Olivia motioned for Ken to come over to Karen's porch and explained the situation. Ken shrugged. "Hey, it would only take me a second to pop that broken window out if you've got the new one."

Karen happily pointed to the new window, where it was stored still in its paper wrappings in the garage.

Within half an hour, Karen had her new window, and Olivia and Ken were back at home having dinner.

Karen was ecstatic. *I can't believe it. It's about time!*

Then her husband, Dave, arrived home. Before he could even set his briefcase down, Karen pulled him over to the new window and pointed, smiling.

Dave took one look. "How . . .?"

So Karen explained how their handy neighbor Ken had installed it in just a few minutes.

Dave's face took on the appearance of a thundercloud. And it stayed that way the rest of the evening.

What is his problem? Karen wondered. *We finally get something done around here, and he gets ticked?*

It wasn't until Karen and I talked about it later that she realized what she'd done. "Ouch." She winced. "I had no idea how much I had hurt his feelings by asking another guy to help me. I just wanted to get it done. If I knew then what I know now, I wouldn't have taken Ken up on the offer."

What's more important to you, ladies? That you get a project done? Or that you wait awhile (even if it seems like forever) and give your husband the opportunity to take care of it?

"Wait a minute there, Dr. Leman!" you might say. "If I did things that way and waited for *my* husband, nothing would ever get fixed in our house!"

If that is your frustration, then talk to him about the situation. Use *I* rather than *you* language. Try this approach: "Honey, I'm wondering if you could take a minute to look at the kitchen sink. It doesn't seem to be working properly, and it would really help me if it could be fixed. Would you mind?"

Approaching your guy in such a way accomplishes the following:

1. You show that you value and respect his opinion.
2. You're asking for his help and saying you need it.
3. You're telling him that you would really *appreciate* the item working. You're honoring his contribution to the family.

If a guy is approached in such a way, how could he refuse?

Here's another tip. Before you add, "Or should I call a repairman?" let him take a real look. Then he will be more likely to say, "You know, I think we need a repairman."

If a man can't fix something himself, he at least wants to be the one to call the repairman, research the repairman, or at least say you need a repairman. No matter that you're the one who will most likely follow through on that repair.

The key is to remember that no man in his right mind is going to admit up front, "I am not capable of fixing that!" By saying so, he would be saying to his own male ego, "I'm a failure. I'm a loser. I can't do anything."

FOR A MAN, THE SYMBOL OF FIXING SOMETHING IS A METAPHOR FOR HIS PROVISION FOR HIS FAMILY.

For a man, the symbol of fixing something is a metaphor for his provision for his family. It hits at the core of who a man is (more on this in the next chapter).

Whether he can do it or not, he needs you—his bride—to believe in him.

Some of you are thinking, *Holy moley! It seems like a wife needs a degree in child psychology to deal with her husband.*

Good! Now you're getting it. Let's move along.

A JUDGMENT CALL

While we're on the subject of home repairs (interestingly enough, many couples get divorced while building or remodeling their home), I want to address another subject: trust.

Many men are handy around the house. I am not. Just ask my wife, Sande. She can read instructions without getting frustrated. I cannot.

But yesterday was an exception for Kevin Leman in the home-improvement department. I was so proud of myself. I walked into the house beaming and called, "Honey! Whaddya know! I fixed something!" Her eyebrows raised, and rightfully so. She had to see it to believe it.

The autofill lever on our swimming pool had been leaking profusely. I was smart enough to figure the thing needed a washer. So off I went to the hardware store and bought two 25-cent washers. I took the autofill lever apart, replaced the washer, and put it all back together. But the leak was still there. I spotted another fitting about 1 ½ inches up toward the end of the contraption, and thought, *You know what? That must come apart.* So I find a wrench/pliers and start to bang on the steel until I get it apart. I find the other leak in there, dig the other washer out of my pocket, screw it on, and . . . voilà! Problem solved.

And *I* did it.

I was so proud of myself for conquering that autofill lever that I wanted to call my buddy Joe and say, "Hey, I fixed something!" He probably would have clutched his heart and fallen over. He knows my record in such an arena.

If Sande was a different kind of woman, she might have responded, "It's about time, you dummy!" But being the patient, wonderful, understanding woman she is, she laughed right along with me and encouraged me in my fix-it skills. (Though she's still wary if she sees me walking around with any tools. . . .)

But many men, handy or not, are "called" to start building or remodeling something in their home.

Like Paul, who got the itch to remodel his bathroom as a present to his wife for their fifteenth anniversary. He was going to convert their ¾ bathroom in the front hallway to a full bathroom by removing the closet. In December and January, he consulted with all his buddies who are in the trades. He spent evening after evening doing the figures to see how much it would cost. By March he was convinced that he could save his family money by doing it himself. He spent two Saturdays gathering the materials for the job.

The next Saturday was his first day on the job. Just as he began tearing out the tile on the wall between the shower and the closet, his wife, Sarah, peered around the corner. "Uh, are you sure you know what you're doing?" she asked.

Paul's frown spoke volumes. He'd done all his homework, bought all the supplies, and she was questioning his judgment?

What was Sarah saying to him by her question? *I don't trust you to do this project.*

YOUR MAN NEEDS TO KNOW THAT YOU TRUST HIM TO MAKE GOOD DECISIONS.

It made Paul feel like he couldn't measure up in her eyes.

Such treatment may trigger a man's temper, but most often he quietly seethes inside and becomes passive-aggressive.

Your man needs to know that you *trust* him to make good decisions. Not that he'll always be right, but he needs to know you will give him the benefit of the doubt (even if you do secretly have the phone number of a home emergency specialist in your wallet!).

WHAT YOUR GUY FEARS THE MOST IN THE WORLD

A woman who suffers from the I-don't-trust-you disease is often a perfectionist in disguise—a critical-eyed person. Even when things are good, she has to find a reason why it could be better. She's continually trying to jump over the high bar of life, then raising it—both on herself and others. At any time, she pulls out her internal measuring stick to check on her husband's progress. Even if he does jump favorably over the bar, she simply pushes the bar higher and tells him, "Try it again." So he keeps jumping higher and higher until the goal is impossible, and he fails.

Then what happens? She rejects him. "You're such a loser. Why did I marry you anyway?"

If you want to stab a man in the heart, reject him. Act like he's worthless. Give him the cold treatment. Don't fulfill him sexually. Because rejection is what every man fears more than anything else. And he fears it most from you, because he cares the most about what you think. He has few friends, yet he has risked letting you into his heart and life. And that's why your rejection hurts him the most. Because men like to appear in control, they are inwardly worried that their weaknesses will be discovered. That they will look inadequate. That they will be rejected.

REJECTION IS WHAT EVERY MAN FEARS MORE THAN ANYTHING ELSE.

Have you ever asked your guy, "Do I look fat in this dress?"

If so, you've put him in a lose-lose situation. He can't win, no matter how he responds. He will most certainly fail in your expectations and be rejected. If he says, "You look great in that," you'll respond, "You're lying. I know I look fat." And no man in his right mind will respond to that question with the truth: "Yes, you really do look fat in that dress. If I were you, I wouldn't wear it to dinner."

You put your guy in a losing situation any time you ask him to comment on your body shape—something women are sensitive about anyway. But let's face it. Neither you nor your guy look the same as you did when you were teenagers.

So why not save those questions for your girlfriends, who are probably bemoaning the same things anyway?

WHAT'S YOURS IS HIS!
You want to bet this is true. When you agreed to marry this man and "to have and to hold" him for a lifetime, everything that was yours became his, and everything that was his became yours. But you might be surprised what he considers "his."

And it doesn't only include your body. It includes your stuff—if there's any that he wants, like your secret stash of chocolate pretzels—anything on your plate, your car keys, and the pile of papers and bills you wish he hadn't looked through.

Allowing him to claim "your stuff" is a symbol of respect in your guy's view. Most especially in the area of food!

QUIZ

Offering your girlfriend's husband your leftover filet mignon at dinner is

A. not a problem. After all, that steak tasted like roadkill, but Phil will eat anything.

B. a kind and thoughtful gesture (Phil still looked hungry).

C. a sure way to cut your fat intake for the day in half.

D. gross. You offered it because he looked so eager but never dreamed he'd take you up on it.

For answers, see page 181.

MULTITASKER EXTRAORDINAIRE

I've said this earlier, but I'll say it again. Women are extraordinarily gifted at juggling multiple tasks simultaneously. That amazes and intimidates us men. In fact, men can feel dissed by their wives' sheer busyness because a woman's life entails myriad relationships and details.

I'm awestruck at the way my wife can juggle eight balls in the air at once, and none of them come tumbling down. I juggle two things at once and get exhausted.

Here's one example. Sande is a wonderful cook, even though when we got married, she couldn't cook a stick. Even more miraculous, when she cooks, she gets everything to come out at the same time! When I cook, I tell the kids, "Okay, everybody get to the table. We're going to have corn." Fifteen minutes later, I call, "Okay, get back to the table. The baked potatoes are ready." Ten minutes after that, "Okay, the chicken's ready!" That's my idea of multitasking. Then there's Sande, who delivers it all to the table *at the same time . . . and steaming hot too.* How she does that is a mystery to me still, after all these years.

Even when she was working at Shabby Hattie and arriving home at 5:30, Sande managed to pull off dinners to die for. Every once in a while I surprised her by cooking dinner. One night I thought, *Hey, her best meal is that fabulous pork tenderloin, and I could do that. Nothing to it!* I knew she poured some kind of soup over it when she baked it in the oven, but I wasn't sure what kind. Because I didn't want her to know what I was up to (remember: I'm the baby of the family, and babies like surprises), I didn't phone her to ask.

I SHOULD HAVE CALLED. I WOULD HAVE SAVED 18 BUCKS ON PORK TENDERLOIN.

In retrospect, I should have called. I would have saved 18 bucks on pork tenderloin. But I was determined to do it all myself. And boy, I should have received an A for effort. I browned the chunk of meat on the stove, then poured the soup over it and placed it in the oven, savoring the heavenly aromas.

When we sat down for dinner, I was feeling good about myself . . . until Sande and the kids got a look at my creation. It looked . . . gross. Sande danced around a few pieces of it but couldn't seem to get it down her throat. The kids just eyed each other, then promptly said they weren't very hungry.

All because I'd poured chicken noodle soup (and not onion soup) over that roast, and when the roast came out of the oven, those little white noodles looked like maggots!

I ate it—all of it. Nobody else would touch it.

I like contributing to my family and helping Sande, but sometimes my efforts don't always turn out well—like that pork tenderloin. It's fortunate that Sande has a great sense of humor and understands how important it is to me, as a man, to try. And not only to try but to have her notice my efforts. That's why, when I'm setting the table for her, I rattle the glasses a little so Sande will know that I'm helping and thank me. Even if I'm not a multitasker extraordinaire, like Sande, I need to be acknowledged for my part in the family.

So does your guy!

THE MAN'S #1 COMMANDMENT

What's the man's #1 commandment? "Thou shalt not diss me."

Your man needs to be respected, he needs to be needed, he needs to be fulfilled. And none of his three basic needs are covered if he feels disrespected.

When guys are dissed, their immediate response is to get quiet. But they are actually roaring inside. Did you ever see the movie *The Lion King* and hear the song lyrics, "In the jungle, the mighty jungle, the lion sleeps tonight"?

Your male lion may look docile, lying around and yawning or

flicking his tail at a fly every once in a while, but beware if you get him angry. He may lie there quietly for a while, but his roar will come out *loudly* later. When you least expect it, he may strike.

Danny had felt dissed for years and had never told his wife, Lauren, how he felt . . . until the big blowup. Danny was an electrician's apprentice, working 55 hours a week to keep his family afloat. When their youngest child went to first grade, Lauren got a job. Quickly she rose to the top as a designer. Within the first year, she was making twice as much as Danny. Every time she brought home a paycheck, he felt dissed. Now it was Lauren who was providing for the family, more than he was. By the second year, they were able to buy a nicer car and move into a three-bedroom home. Their children started attending a private school. But that didn't make Danny any happier.

> YOUR MALE LION MAY LOOK DOCILE, LYING AROUND AND YAWNING OR FLICKING HIS TAIL AT A FLY EVERY ONCE IN A WHILE, BUT BEWARE IF YOU GET HIM ANGRY.

The final straw was when he overheard his son, Troy, boasting to another fourth grader on the playground, "My mommy makes more than your daddy!"

Danny was quiet that night over dinner. After the kids were in bed, he told his wife he was going to run an errand . . . and he didn't come home.

FIGHT FAIR!

Every couple has "those moments" when words come out flying. So when you have to fight, at least fight fair!

1. Remember that fighting is an act of cooperation.
2. Stay on the subject at hand.
3. Don't be a bone digger, bringing up past stuff.
4. Avoid the words *you* and *never*, as in "You never listen to me!"
5. Face each other and hold hands.
6. Have one person talk at a time. Do not interrupt.
7. When one person's done, the other person can respond.
8. After that exchange, clarify only if the issue needs to be clarified (i.e., someone has the wrong perception). Don't kill a dead horse.

9. If things get too hot, call a time out. Kids need recess, and you may too!
10. Don't avoid the topic. After your break, tackle it again the same day. Do not let the sun go down on your anger (Ephesians 4:26).

Later he called her and left a message: "I'm leaving you. You and the kids don't need me anymore. I hope you all have a good life."

Lauren was furious—and shocked. How could he do this? He'd never said anything about being unhappy before. And now he was leaving? *Where did all this come from?* she wondered.

Danny did come back after a week. It took a year of counseling with both Danny and Lauren for them to reconcile the issue. Lauren finally came to understand why Danny was so upset—that she made more money than he did.

> There would be fewer divorces if there were more "no fault" marriages.
>
> —Unknown

I can already hear some of you interjecting a few words of your own. "What's with that? He's such a sexist! He should have been glad that they could buy a bigger house and a better car and send the kids to a private school."

But listen to where Danny was coming from. His father had been a meek individual who always "did what he was told." Danny's mom ran the household . . . and her husband's life. At the age of 53, Danny's father committed suicide. All Danny had left of him was a tattered note that read, *All I wanted was some respect.*

Danny was afraid that if his wife made more than him, she would run the household instead of him.

A lot more was going on in Danny's head and heart than his wife could ever have known!

Am I being a sexist and using this example to say you should quit *your* job if you make more than your husband? Not at all. Ralph and Louise have made that same scenario work—and happily so—for over 25 years. The difference between the couples is what's "behind the story." For Danny, having his wife make more than he did scared and emasculated him. He didn't feel respected or honored in his own home. Even his son knew that his daddy wasn't holding up his end of the bargain.

Ralph was a very confident guy from a stable, loving background.

He and his wife went out to celebrate every time he got a pay raise and every time she got a pay raise!

The apostle Paul was talking to guys when he said, "Each one of you also must love his wife as he loves himself, and the wife must respect her husband."[2]

An interesting choice of words.

A husband is to *love* his wife. And *affection* (translate: love) is her top need!

A wife is to *respect* her husband. And *respect* is his top need!

Mariage is about putting your spouse's needs above your own. And that means choosing to respect your husband, whether or not you agree with him. Respect can't be based on his job (or lack of a job), on whether he succeeds (or fails), but on who he is.

We all would do well to follow his advice.

If you show your man respect, he'll do anything for you. You'll have a true, lifelong, loyal partner.

"MANSPEAK"

WHAT BEST DESCRIBES YOUR GUY?

1. The Lone Ranger riding off into the sunset
2. The turtle wedged under a rock
3. Cave man extraordinaire
4. Other

WE MEN NEVER WANT TO ADMIT WE'RE LOST, INCAPABLE, OR THAT WE NEED YOUR HELP. After all, we're born and raised to be like the Lone Ranger. He didn't have a group of people surrounding him to help him accomplish his business. He was the self-sufficient guy riding off into the sunset. He didn't stop behind the closest rock to consult a map or ask anybody for directions either. He *knew* where he was going (besides, asking for help would have ruined the film).

So how can you get your self-sufficient guy to be on the same rock with you?

Soothe his competitive edge.

Think back to what attracted you to him in the first place. Then write him a note and relive that experience on paper. Tell him how much you respect him. "Honey, I'm so proud of you for all the hard work you've been doing the past week. I know it's exhausting, but I know you can do it!" If he knows he has your respect, his feelings will not be ruffled when you have to tell him sometimes that you don't agree with him or that he messed up.

No human being is always lovable. You certainly aren't—especially at that crabby time of the month. It's not the time we guys choose to approach you about selling the house and moving to the Balkans. Even when you're not feeling lovable, what do you want from your guy? To be loved, right?

What he wants most is your respect. Because that tells him he matters and that his role in your life and in the world matters.

Verbalize your trust in him.

Don't assume he knows you trust him. Verbalize that trust.

Let's say that you two are considering a big decision, like relocating. He needs to hear your thinking and feelings about the move, but he also needs to hear from you, "I trust you. I know you will carefully consider all the options and make the best decisions for your family. I'd love it if you would share your thoughts as you come up with them, because then I can stay on track with what you're thinking."

It's a clever way to say you'd like to be informed as his thoughts form, instead of him "announcing" a decision to you, but that you also trust his gut and his careful planning of your life together.

Should you ask questions sometimes? Certainly! As long as those questions are couched in terms of respect. "I'm hearing what you're saying, and I think you're on the right track. Have you thought about . . . ?" Keep the *buts* out of your conversation and it'll be less touchy.

If you find yourself arguing with your spouse about a decision, it's time to back off, take a time-out, and approach it again later that day (see "Fight Fair!" on pp. 139–140 for some more tips) when you've been able to think through your response instead of just reacting.

Think about it this way: Would you like it if someone argued with you about your day-to-day decisions? Like what you should wear to work? How you should discipline the kids? What groceries you should buy?

Your guy needs your respect and your trust in him.

Ever heard the old adage "What people think of you, you will become"?

YOUR GUY NEEDS YOUR RESPECT AND YOUR TRUST IN HIM.

Learn to read his secret signals.

A man has a hard enough time talking. Add to that the fact that he can't be honest about his thoughts and feelings because he's certain you will either think, *He can't really think that*, or you might get angry about the truth. So we men, like puppies, have learned the right responses. If we sit down and bark appropriately or do tricks, we'll get a treat. If we don't behave, we'll get locked out in the doghouse. We're not stupid enough to risk that!

So if you want to know what we really think, read our body language. Is your guy shuffling his feet, unable to meet your eyes? Then he's feeling uncomfortable with the question. He's even more worried about hurting your feelings. If these are his signals, you may want to back up and say, "Honey, I'm sorry I asked you that. I know it puts you in an uncomfortable position, but what you think is really important to me. I want to be attractive to you. That's what is most important to me."

And then if he responds to your question, take the answer for what it's worth. Don't read into it, don't read behind it, don't read in front of it. Take it for the truth.

"I think you look a little like a bumble bee in that yellow-and-black-striped suit," he might say. "Is there anything else you could wear to my company dinner?"

Realize that what he says is not meant to hurt you (unless you're battling a passive-aggressive guy). It's just the truth, in his eyes. The simple truth.

Take a look back at yourself.

What's the one thing you told yourself you'd never do when you got married? Take a minute to reflect.

Now, let me ask you a question. *Have* you done that very thing? If so, how long did it take before you said the same words or used the same tone or hand gestures as your father did?

How you treat your guy has a lot to do with how much you respected your father.

Here's what I mean. A father promises his young daughter that he will take her out for ice cream after he gets back from the hardware store. The daughter waits by the door for two hours. Eventually Dad does come home, but he smells like alcohol and his speech is slurred. Of course, he forgets all about his promise to take her out for ice cream.

Twenty years later, her husband promises to take her out for dinner. He is legitimately delayed when he gets a flat tire on the way home. When he does finally show up 45 minutes late, his wife reads him the riot act. He can't understand why she is so upset because he doesn't realize she's not just yelling at him—she's yelling at her drunken father.

Early events (when you were in third grade or younger) helped shape your expectations about life and about the way things should be done. You learned either that the world is a safe place . . . or a dangerous place. You developed the assumption that people will either treat you with kindness . . . or betray and threaten you. Because of what was done to you, you learned to make any number of assumptions that as an adult you now take for granted. Is it any surprise that you would view your guy through the lens of your memories?

IS IT ANY SURPRISE THAT YOU WOULD VIEW YOUR GUY THROUGH THE LENS OF YOUR MEMORIES?

Like Cheri, who bristled every time her husband asked, "How was your day?" She'll never forget her father making her account for—in writing—every 10 minutes of her life during her teen years.

What's in your past? How did you relate to your father? What assumptions did you carry with you from your childhood?

As you learn to recognize tendencies based on your history with your father, you'll gain a better understanding of these unspoken assumptions. Until you know what they are, you won't be able to edit them. In cases of abuse, you will need the help of a godly counselor to walk you through your past.

You have to be the one who initiates the look at your past. No one else can begin that process for you. You have to be the one who discovers, evaluates, then comes up with a plan to change your current response.

You'll need to be patient with yourself, for the changes won't happen overnight. But each time you're tempted to respond to your guy as if he were your father and you want to lash back at him, take a breath first. Think, *He is not my father. He deserves my respect.*

Ask God to help you put away the past so you can move on in confidence, loving your husband and meeting his needs.

Strive for mutual respect in your home.

The apostle Paul gave the very best rule for marriage that anyone could ever give in Ephesians 5:21: "Submit to one another out of reverence for Christ." In very traditional or religious homes, much to-do is made over

Ephesians 5:22: "Wives, submit to your husbands as to the Lord." But oftentimes, verse 21 is skipped. Why is that?

I'm convinced it's because so many have a misunderstanding of what was meant by verse 22. Add on verse 25: "Husbands, love your wives, just as Christ loved the church and gave himself up for her," and you've got a better and bigger picture of the meaning of the passage.

In homes that will last, submission is mutual; respect is mutual. Both parties agree that they are equal in God's sight and in each other's sight, but that they are also different from each other. Equal doesn't mean the same.

God has given each of you unique abilities, and that's what makes you a couple. It certainly makes life exciting!

The couple who strives for mutual respect will create the kind of environment in their home where everyone feels safe to express his or her feelings. You don't have to agree, but you do have to hear each other out without interrupting. And you have to respect the thought and the emotion behind the words, even if you have a differing point of view. When such an atmosphere is established, mutual respect reigns in the family, and all will benefit.

> Marriage is a union that can't be organized when both sides think they're management.
>
> —Unknown

MAKE YOUR HOME A REFUGE

1. Use nonthreatening communication. Raising your voice (a nice way to say "yelling") is not tolerated.
2. Keep harshness and rudeness out of your tone.
3. Value his opinion and thoughts, even if they are not as well stated as yours.
4. Stop working and look him in the eyes when he has something to tell you.
5. Allow him to express his feelings, even when they may be more raw or expressed in a more crude manner than you're comfortable with.
6. Choose your battles carefully. Not every little thing is worth fighting over.
7. Laugh together . . . a lot.
8. Pray for each other, and pray together.

Celebrate his successes, even if they seem small to you.

Even if he doesn't do it like you do, thank him for his efforts. Encourage him the first time he changes a diaper. "Oh, honey, you did it! Those

Pampers can be tricky to get on the right way, but you did it! And look how happy she is. What a great daddy you are."

It may seem like a small thing to you for him to change one diaper a day when he gets home from work, but to him it's a big thing. He's contributing to the family and doing it in a way that is entirely out of his realm of experience. I can vouch for the fact that most guys have no clue you *never* check a diaper from behind unless you want mustard-tipped fingers!

If something was out of your realm of experience, how would you want to be treated?

It all comes back, once again, to the Golden Rule: "Treat others as you yourself would want to be treated."

That's what makes a marriage go 'round.

#7

THING HE'LL NEVER TELL YOU

"I'd take a bullet for you."

Why your man longs not only to be a hero, but your hero.

● ● ●

IF YOU MADE a list of your real-life heroes, who would be on that list?

I will never forget seeing the firemen running into the burning World Trade Center and the Pentagon on September 11, 2001. They were risking their lives to save others, people they didn't even know, and many of them died that day. Yes, those men were in a job that called for putting their lives on the line, but that day—and in the days to follow—those New York City firemen went beyond the call of duty.

There were others, such as Todd Beamer, who knew he would die for such an action but chose to rush the terrorists on United Flight 93—the only terrorist-guided plane on 9/11 that didn't hit its intended target. Did Todd wake up that day saying, "I'm going to be a hero?" Certainly not. He boarded what he thought would be a normal business flight. Yet his final words on earth, "Let's roll!" became the rallying cry of a nation.[1]

I remember turning to my wife that day, as we sat stunned and horrified, and saying in a choked-up voice, "Now those are *real men.*"

Those men (and women) made the supreme sacrifice. They knocked down walls to rescue people with little or no thought to the risk they were taking themselves. They risked their own physical safety on board a plane to put others first.

Do you have any idea, ladies, how much your husband wants to be your hero? How he *needs* to be your hero? For you, he would knock down a wall with gusto and not worry about the peril to himself.

LONGING TO BE YOUR HERO IS WHAT DRIVES YOUR MAN.

Longing to be your hero is what drives your man. It's what makes him work the long hours and put up with that long commute. It's why he boards the plane every Wednesday and doesn't come back until Friday. There are parameters around how sold out his soul is to his company. But you? If he feels respected, needed, and fulfilled by you, there are no holds barred. He would do anything. He would take a bullet for you.

IF HE FEELS RESPECTED, NEEDED, AND FULFILLED BY YOU, THERE ARE NO HOLDS BARRED. HE WOULD DO ANYTHING. HE WOULD TAKE A BULLET FOR YOU.

Because that's what a real man does . . . and how he becomes a hero in the eyes of the woman he loves.

HE WANTS TO BE YOUR OWN PERSONAL JAMES BOND

If you've seen any James Bond flicks, you know what to expect. Even in the midst of adventure, danger, and intrigue, James Bond always has time to woo a lady. And his ladies aren't wimpy creatures either. Most of them can stand on their own two feet—and put you in your place too.

I can relate. I love Italian-American families. I grew up with them in New York. The men may act like they run the family, but the reality is that the *women* run the family. They just allow the men to feel like they do!

I GREW UP WITH ITALIANS IN NEW YORK. THE MEN MAY ACT LIKE THEY RUN THE FAMILY, BUT THE REALITY IS THAT THE WOMEN RUN THE FAMILY. THEY JUST ALLOW THE MEN TO FEEL LIKE THEY DO!

QUIZ

Why it's difficult for your man to be your hero

A. Because you do everything so well—and do it all.

B. You're so busy.

C. You don't stand still long enough for him to help or to please you.

D. Because he's afraid that you'll find fault with whatever he does.

For answers, see pages 181–182.

There's a misconception among many that men want helpless women. Rhonda fell into that trap. She was 38, not yet married but longing to be. For over 10 years she had wanted to buy a house—a yellow house—and plant a garden. But year after year she stayed in an apartment because she was afraid if she looked too self-sufficient, no guy would ever want her. She thought he'd be scared of her independence.

But a healthy man doesn't want a helpless woman. He desires a capable woman who has a sense of independence and self-sufficiency, yet is still vulnerable and needs rescuing every once in a while.

He wants to be your own live-action James Bond, leaping tall buildings for you and zooming off to your rescue. He needs you to depend on him. He wants to provide for you. He craves your respect and admiration. And, yes, he wants you to respond to him sexually with the fervor of a James Bond woman. He wants you to be excited *and* exciting in bed.

Your man may not be the top dog at work, he may

Aggression is part of the masculine *design;* we are hardwired for it.

—John Eldredge,

Wild at Heart[2]

not have the fastest car, he may be losing what few looks he had to begin with, his hair may be falling out while his gut is growing, but if his honey loves him in every way, he will feel young again. He'll take on the world—that troublesome boss, a difficult vocational challenge, or that seemingly closed job market—one more time. Twenty firms may have rejected him, but if the man has a loving wife at home, he'll retreat every evening after his job search to his own personal island of love. He'll be recharged enough to wake up the next day to visit 20 more firms.

The fulfillment that he gets at work doesn't pack even one ounce of the emotional punch that your whispered words, "James, I love you . . . I need you . . ." do.

As John Eldredge says, "There is nothing so inspiring to a man as a beautiful woman. She'll make you want to charge the castle, slay the giant, leap across the parapets. . . . A man wants to be the hero to the beauty."[3]

HE SOMETIMES WALKS THE BALANCE BEAM . . . AND FALLS OFF

Every time I see the gymnasts at the Olympics, I marvel. Exactly how do they mount and do all those exercises on a balance beam the width of a two-by-four? Gymnasts have incredible balance, strength, and determination. My body hurts just watching the guys on the rings who hold their entire bodies up by the strength in their arms!

But even real heroes get the worst of life and fall off the balance beam occasionally. Sometimes your real-life hero needs your help and encouragement to get back on.

I got a phone call last week from a desperate 54-year-old man. After his company downsized and his position was cut, he had spent three months looking for work, and the last six months driving semis cross-country. In that time, he had seen his kids for only 14 days. He and his family were merely trying to survive. He was embarrassed, deep down, that his wife had to sign up for food stamps. "I just wonder if life is worth living any more," he said. "I can't even provide for my family."

Another couple, Bill and Kristine, had married later in life. They were both 50 and had two adolescent children. Kristine worked part-time as a teacher, and her husband's job paid the bills. Then he lost his job and had difficulty finding a new one at his age. Kristine picked up the slack. She took a full-time teacher position and was able to get health coverage as well. But her husband was devastated. There was no way their family could live on her small salary; it barely covered their house payment.

Somehow they managed to make it for three months on their slim savings. By the fourth month, though, their refrigerator and pantry shelves were bare.

One afternoon, friends of theirs, Evan and Rebecca, showed up with a carload of groceries. Bill, a tough, stocky guy, stood at the door and wept. "It is so hard for me to receive this," he said. "I have never asked for charity. I'm not a slacker. What can I do for you?"

You see, Bill *needed* to do something for the family who helped him. They gave him groceries, but he needed to provide something in return. So that afternoon, he went to Evan and Rebecca's home and helped Evan cut up a tree in his backyard that had fallen in a storm. By the end of the afternoon, the tree was cut into firewood-size pieces. Another change had taken place, too. Instead of a defeated look, Bill was smiling. There was a new spring in his step.

Two days later Kristine called Rebecca and said, "Thank you for giving Bill back his manhood. He's smiling again and has decided to try job hunting in a different direction."

Life today is uncertain. One guy I know had 25 years with Radio Shack, until they closed a huge number of stores due to stiff competition. Imagine—you have spent a quarter of a century with a company, then the store closes and you are no longer employed! Good old Radio Shack notified thousands of people through e-mail that they were history with the company.

THE QUESTIONS A WOMAN ASKS HERSELF EVERY DAY

- Does he love me?
- Does he love me?
- Does he love me?

THE QUESTIONS A MAN ASKS HIMSELF EVERY DAY

- Does she respect me, or take me for granted?
- Does she understand how much I need to be her hero?
- Does she know how fulfilled I feel when I can provide what I want to provide for my family—and how it hurts me inside when I can't?

When life throws your man a curve, who does he turn to? His buddies? The Chicago Bears he loves to watch? No, he turns to you. But if you're too busy to listen to what he has to say, or too scared to listen to what he has to say (because you may be thinking, *He wants to change jobs? Move across the country? I can't pick up and move like that!*), he will bury himself in his work. Worst of all, you will miss seeing your hero's heart.

It's crucial for a man to know that, even though he may be inadequate at some things, he still has your respect and belief in him as a provider. A man gets his psychological jollies from providing for his family—it's part of his God-given drive that needs to be fulfilled.

That's why a man, even more than a woman, fears losing or changing jobs. The Lone Ranger mentality is so strong that it's emasculating for a man to admit he's "lost"—whether for directions, in his career, in his relationship with you, or in any other area of his life.

It's why more women go to counseling sessions than men. It takes a long time and a lot of humility for a guy to admit, "I need help!" That's why you, the love of his life, may need to offer him that gentle nudge toward healing.

That healing begins with your belief in him and your undying trust that, even in the toughest of times, he and you will make it.

IT TAKES A LONG TIME AND A LOT OF HUMILITY FOR A GUY TO ADMIT, "I NEED HELP!"

HE NEEDS YOUR COMPLETE TRUST

Once in a while I listen to the Top 40 radio station in Tucson. One morning I heard a program they call *The War of the Roses*. It's a scam program, where a radio-station employee phones a guy, says that they are giving away free flowers—no strings attached—and asks who to send the flowers to. The scam is that the guy's wife or girlfriend is behind the call. She doesn't trust him and wants to know if he's cheating on her.

"All you've got to do," the radio employee tells the guy, "is tell us who they are to be sent to . . . and then recommend our wonderful service."

This particular morning, the program had a husband on the phone. "Great!" he said. "Send them to my secretary."

"You know these are red roses, right?" the radio employee asked. "Romantic roses?"

"That's okay," the husband said. "Today is her birthday, so this will be perfect."

"Okay, sir. What would you like to say on the card?"

"Just put Happy Birthday . . . and that's all."

"Wait a minute!" the guy's wife yelled from where she was inside the radio-station studio. "You're not going to send them to me?"

The husband was understandably confused about where the new voice was coming from. So he answered, "No, please send them to my secretary. Thanks."

The woman was furious. She got on the phone and said, "When it's my birthday, you don't send me flowers. And now, even when they're free, you won't send me flowers! What is wrong with you?"

For the next 10 minutes, the wife accused him of having an affair, lambasting him for not being affectionate to her, and accusing him with, "You're just like every other guy I've known. A loser!"

After her long diatribe, how did the man respond? With a sad, "You know we just don't do those things, honey. Like give each other roses."

He was a normal guy—sort of a geek, but a hardworking, responsible, loyal husband who had a good job and provided well for his wife. At one point he said he had to get back to work and ended by saying, "I love you. We'll have to talk about this later." And he hung up.

How he could love that woman, I had no idea. She was a real piece of work.

Finally, after more discussion, the woman admitted to the radio-station personnel that she was having an affair and she had thought her husband was too.

In response to that conversation, radio callers reacted with, "What is wrong with that woman?"

Day by day, that husband was quietly being a hero, providing for a woman who didn't appreciate him and who didn't trust him.

It made me want to weep, for without trust, there can be no relationship.

> Climb inside a guy's mind . . .
>
> *Why would I send my wife flowers? They just die! What would that say about our relationship?*
>
> —Anonymous

WITHOUT TRUST, THERE CAN BE NO RELATIONSHIP.

Then there are couples like Kaye and Rich. Kaye has been wheel-chair-bound with MS for the past three years. Rich is an active cycler and racquetball player. He just turned in his resignation to his boss yesterday. "I want to spend more time with Kaye," Rich told his boss. "She is my reason for living."

There is such trust, loyalty, honor, and respect in their relationship in the midst of Kaye's illness that all who see their sweet interactions marvel and count their own blessings.

HE'S AN EVERYDAY HERO

I was drinking my coffee one day at home and overhearing the chatter between my wife, Sande; my daughter Krissy; and Debbie, my assistant. They were talking about going out for lunch together.

"I gotta go," I told them and headed out the door for work. But on the way, I happened to drive by the restaurant where they were going to have lunch. On a whim, I pulled in and found the maître d' of the place.

"My wife is coming here for lunch at 12:30. She has reservations for three, plus a baby. I'd like to pay for her lunch," I announced.

The maître d' looked at me as if I had a screw loose.

"I'd like you to just swipe my card while I'm here, so I can pay for her lunch. Then tell her that her lunch is already paid for."

"Very well," the maître d' said and swiped my card, then continued to study me with that are-you-really-all-right-in-the-head stare as she waited for my card to process.

Just then a waitress called her away for a minute. The two women began to talk. Sixty seconds later, the waitress walks over to me. Her order pad is clasped against her chest, and tears are streaming down her cheeks. "Oh, I just heard what you were doing, and I had to tell you: that is so sweet!"

I shuffled my feet (the male thing to do when you don't know what to say). "I just thought it would be nice to take care of my sweetie."

It wasn't until I was a couple of miles down the road that it hit me: that waitress had probably never experienced affection or love in her life. Likely she didn't have a kind father or a man who had ever loved her as she was. That had to be why my action affected her so much.

We take so much for granted in marriage, don't we?

Heroes can do big things—like rescue you out of a burning building. But they also do the smaller things. Like making all the phone calls for repair work on your car. Or cleaning your pet bird's cage (when he doesn't even like birds) to give you a break. Or buying you your favorite bath soak "just because" he thought you'd enjoy a break after some hectic deadlines. Or calling State Farm for the second time in a month after you've scraped the same telephone pole. (If I could just get her to stop when she hits something, it would save me thousands.) Or taking your daughter out to shoot arrows into hay bales at the neighbors' to give you time to prepare for her surprise birthday party.

He'll show up, night after night, for Little League. He'll take your daughter to the store to buy a new fish when hers dies. He'll run to the store at 10 p.m. to get Midol and tampons when it's that time of the month and you've run out. (And he'll pray the whole time he's in the store that no one will yell, "Price check!" in the checkout lane.)

He'll also be the family funeral director. In our house, we have buried just about everything you can imagine, including a dog, fish, cats, and rodents. One father told me, "I saw no problem with standing over the toilet bowl to give the fish a burial at sea with a royal flush send-off until I saw my daughter, red eyed and crying. It made me go out and find a burial place in the yard. We even made a cross with twigs and a rubber band to put over the fish's resting spot."

Your hero is honored by helping out at such an emotional time, and glad to be the guardian of your and your children's (especially your daughter's) emotions.

If you follow through on his basic needs and fill his love tank, he'll be the happiest guy on the planet. He'll be steel on the outside, protecting you physically and emotionally, and velvet on the inside, soft toward you, tender with the kids, and intimately involved in your family's life.

Listen to what St. Paul's words say in Ephesians 5: "Husbands, love your wives, just as Christ loved the church and gave himself up for her."[4] To a man, that means, "I'd die for you. I'll be your hero. I'll protect you. I'll share your concerns, fears, and tears (even if I don't always 'get' them)."

REAL MEN ARE . . . WELL, *REAL*

Real men spit, scratch, and argue with you. They get grumpy when you leave the refrigerator door open . . . again. They roll their eyes when you back the car through the garage door.

They sometimes play possum—especially in the middle of the night when a baby is crying. And on other nights, they say magnanimously, "Don't worry, I'll get up and rock the baby."

They don't notice things for a very long time. Over the summer, my wife purchased an ornate fountain that features angels. It sat around all summer because we needed to get somebody to help us hang it on an outside wall of our house.

One September day, as I arrived home, Sande greeted me enthusiastically. Her hands were clasped together in a devout prayer position underneath her chin, and she was stomping her feet like she was really excited (either that, or she needed to use the restroom and I needed to get out of her way). Moving her hands to rest on one side of her cheek, she lay her face down against them, as if they were a pillow, and sighed happily. "Did you see it? What did you think?"

"Uh, what are you talking about?" I say.

"The fountain!"

"I didn't see the fountain."

Sande eyed me. "How could you miss the fountain?"

She marches me out to where it's hanging on the wall. Yep, I sure did miss it. I'm not sure how, though, since it's about six feet high and four and a half feet wide. But I'm sure I would have noticed it, had she put on the wall right beside it Mickey Mantle's trading card. Then I would have been all over it!

Most of us real men are decoration challenged. We're color-blind. We're allergic to doing laundry.

We gladly hear the secrets of your heart, but sometimes we just grunt in response. (However, that doesn't mean that we haven't taken in every word that you've said.)

If you respect, need, and fulfill us, we'll play Monster every night with the kids and love it. Even if we don't have a good-paying job or aren't happy doing what we're doing, we'll catch the kids at night and pretend to salt and pepper them. Then we'll pretend to take a bite of their bellies for dinner.

The woman hearing and observing this will be smiling, saying to herself, *I'm so glad I married that folically challenged man. He's gained 19 pounds and that doesn't matter a bit. He sure does love me and the kids!*

You see, something wonderful happens when you fulfill your man's top three needs. That man will take a bullet for you. He will stand his ground and go to bat for you . . . always.

But he will also *live for you.* He'll vacuum for you without you asking when your mother arrives for her "surprise" visit. He'll want to share your heart. He'll want to know what your deepest desires are . . . and he'll want to help fulfill them. He'll want to please you—the most important person in his life—in every way possible.

He'll be a man like my son-in-law, Dennis. When two of Sande's and my daughters, Krissy and Holly, decided to do a "sister thing" and go to a University of Arizona game together, Dennis had care of little Conner (almost three), and Adeline (one year). I was flying in that day, so I met Sande, Dennis, and the grandbabies later. When I saw Adeline, I couldn't help but notice peaches all over her face and nose. You could tell Dennis had had an interesting few hours while Mommy was at the game. But all three were smiling and happy.

I could tell that day that Dennis was exhausted being a daddy. But he was doing a great job juggling the multiple tasks of caring for two very active little ones.

I couldn't help but look at him and think, *Here is one of the heroes of the next generation. Boy, Krissy knows how to pick 'em, doesn't she?*

For right in front of me I saw an everyday hero in action. And I couldn't have been more proud of him . . . even if my granddaughter's face did need a good washing!

> Winning is finding and implementing a solution that both people can feel good about. In healthy relationships, everyone wins.
>
> —Dr. Gary Smalley, *The DNA of Relationships*[5]

"MANSPEAK"

A REAL HERO

1. acts in love, putting others before himself.
2. considers you as an equal partner but with differing and wonderful gifts.
3. is supportive, not jealous of success in his family.
4. is consistent every day—not only in the large picture but in the small things.

SOCIETY TELLS US THE WOMAN IS THE CENTERPIECE of the American marriage. She's the one who pulls everything and everyone together. But research says that as the man goes, so goes the family.

THE MAKING OF A HERO . . . AND HIS HEROINE

Your man needs to be your hero. And he needs you to be his heroine. Here's how you can make his dream come true—and yours in the process!

Reshape your perspective.

I'd like to ask you a question—a strange, startling question. If you just learned that you had stage 4 ovarian cancer and had roughly six months to live, how would you live your life?

My guess is that suddenly the minutiae of life would pale. The decorations for the fall gala would no longer be as important. The deadlines a month from now wouldn't seem like your top priority. The Sunday school class you agreed to teach next spring would be checked off your to-do list.

What questions would run through your mind about your relationship with your guy?

1. What do I need to say to him before it's too late?
2. What have I said no to that I need to say yes to?
3. If I died tomorrow, would he know I love him, or would he wonder?

After you reflect on the above questions, ask yourself, "How could I incorporate what I've learned into my life now? What should I do differently? How should my life change to reflect these priorities?"

Three weeks ago, when I was in Tacoma, speaking at a conference, a woman approached me at the end of a book signing. "I want you to know you really got my attention last night. And this morning you sealed the deal." She hung her head. "I had my escape route all figured out. As soon as my husband left for work on Friday, I had a moving company coming with a van. The house was going to be cleared out before my husband got home from work. I was just going to leave him a note that I was gone. But you gave me hope that I could try again."

Life is so short. Don't wait. Why not reshape your perspective now, while you have time?

WHAT KIND OF LEADER?

With that in mind, what kind of leader is your guy?

_____ Loving but firm
_____ Dictatorial
_____ Not a leader at all. More of a wimp.

If you checked "Loving but firm," chances are good that your husband grew up in a home where there was social equality between men and women, but both partners functioned differently. His mom was comfortable in her role as a woman; his dad was comfortable in his role as a man and provided loving leadership. His dad was probably your husband's hero, and he has a good relationship with his mom that transfers over to the way he treats you. Your husband has a good understanding of Ephesians 5:21: "Submit to one another out of reverence."

Your marriage is in a great place! Each of you has your own unique abilities and tasks, and you trust each other to do them. Because you are both comfortable with who you are, you don't face the "spirit of competition" that many married couples do.

If you checked "Dictatorial," chances are good that your husband grew up in a home where Dad ruled the roost with an iron fist. Mom was caught between Dad and the children, and her opinion didn't count for much. She was always overruled, and so were you. The only one who mattered was Dad (when he was home). Your husband probably couldn't wait to get out from under his thumb . . . but then became just like his dad when he married you—even more so, if children are involved. His translation of Ephesians 5:21: "Submit, woman, because I am the almighty king of this house, and anything I say goes!"

If this is your man, you have to learn to stand up for what you feel is right. Marriage should be *mutual* submission, with each thinking first of what is best for the other. Your guy may—and probably will—get angry if you assert yourself. But you need to respect yourself enough not to be his doormat.

If you checked "Not a leader at all. More of a wimp," chances are good that your husband grew up in a home where Mom ruled the roost and told the rooster what to do. Dad just went along with things so he wouldn't rock the boat. That meant your husband didn't grow up with a strong male image in his household and may struggle with where a male fits in the family. His laissez-faire attitude may have everything to do with his not knowing how to be a servant leader. His translation of Ephesians 5:21: "I will submit to my wife so I won't get her or anybody else upset. Anything's fine with me."

If this is your man, you're going to have to work hard to include him. Ask him what he thinks, tell him his opinion is important to you. Reaffirm his role in the family as the leader, and slowly begin to defer some decisions to him that he wouldn't normally make.

Encourage, but don't praise.

Have you ever felt uncomfortable when someone praised you? Why do you think that is?

It's probably because many times praise feels false. And it is false. "Oh, Jennifer, I just love the way you do your hair!" "Kevin, you did such an awesome job on that song!" The reality is, Jennifer's hair looks ridiculous—your four-year-old could have done a better job cutting it—and Kevin didn't play a single note in tune on his trumpet.

But encouragement is different. "John, I appreciate so much you taking the extra time to pick up dinner on a stressful day for me." And, "The flowers you sent me for no reason made me feel so loved. How do you always know when I need it? Here's a great big hug and kiss . . . and there's more to come later!"

In short, praise takes away from the heart. Encouragement takes it to the heart.

How can you encourage your man today? Notice him, admire him, and appreciate him. But do it with real encouragement, not fake praise.

Pray together and for each other.

My colleague John Trent reports on the results of a study on married couples and prayer. Couples who pray 3-4 times a week together only have a divorce rate of 1 in 1,052. I had to replay the tape a few times to make sure I heard that right. (Note that George Barna's research claims that those who believe in God and that those who don't have about the same divorce rate. So it's not just *belief* or *faith* that will help you sustain your marriage, but *praying together and for each other.*)

Compare those figures with the national average, and it really makes you think. Most married partners have the "married single" lifestyle: you do things independently, so there's not enough that you share with your husband to keep the relationship going after a while.

But when you are drawn together emotionally, physically, *and* spiritually, it is rare for that bond to break!

> The best marriages are a blending of two people. While each person maintains his and her unique personality and interests, they both deliberately integrate those interests. When it's done right, each person becomes a happier and better person.
>
> —Willard F. Harley Jr.,
> *His Needs, Her Needs for Parents*[6]

PRAISE TAKES AWAY FROM THE HEART.
ENCOURAGEMENT TAKES IT TO THE HEART.

If you want to hear what's in your husband's heart, to know what's on his mind, pray with him. It may be uncomfortable at first if you're not used to it, but the rewards in your relationship will be phenomenal.

Base your home firmly on your faith.

The Old Testament leader Joshua, speaking near the end of his life, was adamant about his faith and how it affected his family and home life. "But as for me and my household, we will serve the LORD."[7]

If someone took a good look at your DayTimer or sat in on a family discussion, what would those things say about whom you are serving? Do you serve yourself? others? God?

All of us serve someone. Who is most important to you? And how does your life reflect that priority?

A three-strand rope—God, you, your family—is not easily broken.[8]

And in today's world, that's something wonderful to hold on to.

> Submit to one another out of reverence.
>
> —Ephesians 5:21

CONCLUSION

Talking His Language

If you understand his basic needs and talk in ways he understands,
you'll be well on your way to the relationship of your dreams!

• • •

We've just spent a whole book talking about what makes your guy tick,
what ticks him off, and how you can make your relationship satisfying
and fulfilling for both of you.

Now that you know a man's three basic needs—to
be respected, needed, and fulfilled—where do you go
from here? How can you act on the 7 things you've
learned that he'd never tell you but you need to know?
What's the best way to talk your man's language?[1]

THAT'S AMORÉ!

I'll be blunt. Even though I'm a psychologist, there are
very few books in the field of applied psychology that
I consider worth reading. But one of them was written
by a colleague of mine, Gary Chapman. His wonderful book, *The Five Love Languages,* has caused many
trees to give up their life. But I highly recommend this

> Everything in
> life that truly
> matters can be
> boiled down to
> relationships.
>
> —Dr. Gary Smalley,
>
> *The DNA of*
>
> *Relationships*

brilliant work. It has given so many of us a "handle" for understanding how we—and those we love—give and receive love best.[2]

This concept is particularly important, I believe, in the area of male-female relationships. Especially where you already have so many innate differences.

But how can you discover your guy's love language?

It's unlikely that he'll wake up in the morning, thinking, *I can't wait to tell her what my love language is.* You'll have to discover it. But it's easier than you think. Simply listen to what he complains about! "You never . . ." or "You always . . ." or "I don't get to . . ." Men are known to whine like little puppies when their feet are stepped on.

People express their love in different ways, Gary Chapman says. And they expect to receive love in that same way. If you don't understand that unspoken expectation, it can cause problems in your relationship. But as you identify your own love language and your man's love language, you can learn to speak a common language that will bring a greater fulfillment and joy to your marriage.

Here's a peek at the five love languages. See if you can identify your own . . . and also your man's.

Words of affirmation

The people who use this love language tend to be verbal, at ease with words. They express themselves well. They use words of affirmation to uplift others. They excel at paying sincere compliments and offering encouraging words. They always have something nice to say about your appearance, talents, achievements, or attitude.

The downside to this love language is that those who have this love language also expect kind words in return. They can feel neglected when they don't hear similar affirming words from their mates. They can also overdo their compliments, and then the words don't mean as much. Nonverbal people don't trust words as much as verbal people, so they can read insincerity or sarcasm into all sorts of innocent comments.

Quality time

The people who use this love language love doing things together—going on trips, going out to dinner, rollerblading, backpacking. Willard Harley calls it "recreational companionship"—doing the things you love to do with the person you love to do them with. It's like *dat-*

ing, when you think about it—something many busy couples forget to do after their wedding date.

But note that there's a difference between simply taking up space next to someone on the couch, and really *engaging* with that person. Giving him or her your full attention.

I can identify with this love language, because it's mine. Any time I can get alone with Sande, I'm a happy dude. The problem is, those moments don't happen enough. If I want quality time with my wife, with all that goes on in my house, I have to go to the master bedroom and bolt and lock the door in four places. Sometimes you have to fight for your quality time!

Gifts

To people who use this love language, "gifts are visual symbols of love," says Chapman.[3] These folks love to give gifts . . . and they do it lavishly. Giving doesn't have to be expensive to be lavish. A wildflower picked from the roadside can mean as much as a diamond bracelet. It's more a matter of involvement, of interest, of care.

The flip side of a gift giver is that he or she can be hurt if you don't show appreciation for that gift.

Sande is a gift giver. She *invents* reasons to give gifts to people. The night before we're having friends over, she'll be baking little heart-shaped cookies to place in party favors that our guests can take home (remember "the bags" she had to run back into the house to get?).

I don't have the same gift-giving nature. I figure we're already giving them dinner; why can't *I* eat the cookies?

Acts of service

People who use this love language see love in terms of *doing things for others.* And that means things beyond the "normal expectation" of duties. But here's the problem. Most couples haven't quite agreed on "what's normal" regarding jobs in the house, so how can they know what's extra? For example, she may always prepare dinner, but tonight she makes his favorite dessert. That's extra. He may always clean the bathroom, but today he cleans the kitchen too, so she doesn't have to. That's extra. That's an act of service.

Here's the catch on this love language. Many men are service challenged. Perhaps it's because we live in a culture where women do two-thirds of the work. So if your guy has this love language of acts of service, bless you, and bless him!

Physical touch

People who use this love language value the power of touch—kisses, holding hands, bear hugs, back rubs. That's how they show love, and that's how they love to receive it.

I know this love language well. Ask my wife. I'm a toucher, and I love to be a touchee. That's how I show love and how I like to receive it.

QUIZ

What is your guy's love language?

A. Words of affirmation

B. Quality time

C. Gifts

D. Acts of service

E. Physical touch

For answers, see page 182.

What is most important to you?

A. Hearing "I love you, honey" verbally or in a card.

B. Spending relaxed time with your man—just the two of you.

C. Getting flowers not for a special occasion but just because he loves you.

D. When he cleans the bathroom for you and it's not even his turn.

E. Getting a kiss every time he walks in or out of the door.

For answers, see page 182.

BRIDGING THE LANGUAGE GAP

Can you have more than one love language? Definitely. I'm both a quality-time and a physical-touch-love-language kind of guy. Sande is a gift giver and an acts-of-service kind of gal.

We're as different as we could possibly be. Yet we've learned how to make our love languages work beautifully together.

You can, too. Here's an example of how it can work:

Let's say your love language is acts of service. Your husband's is physical touch and words of affirmation. The next time you catch him doing something wonderful—like cutting the grass, when it's your turn—look him in the eye, rub his back, hug him, and tell him how much that means to you.

Because you've touched him and told him how much that meant, he'll be like a happy golden retriever, wagging his tail for you. He'll even sit up, roll over, and bark the next time you want something done.

All you have to do is encourage him, give him strokes, affection, hugs, tell him he's a good boy, and put yummy dog chow and water in his dish every day. If you do these simple things, he'll be the happiest dog in the world!

Hmm. It's amazing how similar men are to golden retrievers . . . and how simple our needs really are.

So why not identify what love language(s) each of you has? Then use that revelation to spur on some conversations between the two of you on how you can show each other love *in the best way you can understand and receive it.*

IT'S AMAZING HOW SIMILAR MEN ARE TO GOLDEN RETRIEVERS . . . AND HOW SIMPLE OUR NEEDS REALLY ARE.

CHANGING . . . WHO?

Women spend billions of dollars a year covering up blemishes and flaws. You've probably got enough war paint in your bathroom drawers to cover anything that ails your face. You are an expert at cover-up.

I've always wondered why the makeup is called Cover Girl. Shouldn't it be called Cover-Up Girl?

But when it gets right down to it, you know all that makeup may help you catch a man, but it won't necessarily help you keep a man. The reality is that you long for the kind of man who will love you when you're grouchy, when you've misbehaved or backed the car into a light pole, when you've said something unkind, or when you have morning breath that would kill a cockroach. You long for the kind of man who says, "Honey, I love you at this time of the month, love you after that time of the month, and love you 10 days before that time of the month."

That man you married, imperfect as he is, is your gift from God. Will you choose to protect, honor, respect, and love that gift, or will you trash it by your words, attitude, and actions?

I'VE ALWAYS WONDERED WHY THE MAKEUP IS CALLED COVER GIRL. SHOULDN'T IT BE CALLED COVER-UP GIRL?

You can read all the shrinky books from Dr. Phil to Oprah's newest hot book, and still the books won't do you a jack diddly-squat of good unless they tell you, *Okay, so you want to change his behavior? Then change your own!*

If we're honest, we have to admit that it's much easier to point a finger at someone else than it is to turn your hand around and point the accusing finger at yourself. Very few people will pony up to the bar and say, "Hey, this is my doing, and I accept responsibility for it."

OKAY, SO YOU WANT TO CHANGE HIS BEHAVIOR? THEN CHANGE YOUR OWN!

But marriage is a two-way street. Each partner is responsible for his own behavior. That means it is *your* decision to think and act differently—in a way that shows your man that you respect him, need him, and want to fulfill him.

If you want to change behavior in yourself, stop and ask, "Given the situation right now, what would I normally do?" Then think through those actions. Ask yourself, "With that in mind, and knowing that I'm trying to change, what should I do next?"

The kicker is that sometimes you won't feel like doing that next step. Who of us does? We're all creatures of habit. When a woman remarries for the third time, she tells herself that she's got a new Ford. She's wrong. She's got the same old Ford. It may have a different paint job, different tires, but the engine she brought home is basically the same. That's why I always tell people it's easier to overhaul what you've got (yourself, as well as your mate), and make it in your first marriage.

A funny thing happens when you start treating yourself, your man, and your marriage in a healthy manner: Your feelings catch up to your actions! When you change your behavior to help your marriage stay on a smooth course, you allow your mate the freedom to change his behavior because he *wants to change* instead of being *forced to change.*

Last week I was in Atlanta, Georgia. Whenever I go to a city to speak, I'm often assigned an escort who will drive me from my hotel to the meeting site and make sure my needs are met (translation: so that I don't get lost from point A to point B). Anyway, Billy and I had a wonderful time bonding over breakfast at a Waffle House. He's a typical Southern gentleman, a successful businessman who drives around in his GMC SUV. He and his wife both attended the meetings where I spoke.

At the conclusion of my speaking, Billy drove me to the airport. "Dr. Leman," he said, "I really learned something about my wife from you. Do you remember when I brought you a bottle of water at the podium as you spoke?"

I nodded. "Sure do. That was great."

"Well, here's the reason I did it. As I was listening to you talk, my wife whispered to me, 'Is that your water?' I had it sitting down near my feet. I nodded, and went back to listening to you. A couple of minutes later she whispered to me, 'He sounds parched.'"

Billy laughed. "Doc, before your talk last night, I wouldn't have done a thing in response to that question. But I remembered what you said. Women want us to be able to read their minds. That's one of the ways they feel loved. They want us to understand what they mean . . . even if they're not saying it. When my wife asked me, 'Is that your water?' she gave me clue #1. But it merely made me wonder, *Does she want a sip?* But when she said that you sounded parched, that was clue #2. And I knew what my job as a husband was—to run the water up to you."

Billy got it. Indeed he *had* learned something.

In that small way, he was telling his wife, "You are my number one priority in life. What is important to you is important to me."

What is important to your guy? How will you meet his three top needs? How will you respond to the 7 things he'll never tell you . . . but you need to know?

A healthy, happy, marital relationship is based upon pleasing each other, being sensitive and tuned in to each other's emotional and sexual needs, sharing intimate thoughts and feelings, and understanding the different languages in which you both express your love.

A HEALTHY, HAPPY MARITAL RELATIONSHIP . . . IS THE WORK OF A LIFETIME.

It's the work of a lifetime. But oh, the benefits!
The satisfying partnership awaits you, so plunge right in!
Your own personal hero awaits. . . .

THE TOP 10 MARRIAGE ADVICE LIST

#10 The key to understanding a husband is decoding his grunts.

#9 Life is 10 percent what you make it and 90 percent how you take it.
—Irving Berlin

#8 Guys *need* to be in control of the television remote. Just let him have it.

#7 Have "spaces" in your togetherness. Boys need time to be boys, and girls need time to be girls, without the other sex looking over their shoulders.

#6 Those who pull on the oars together don't have time to rock the boat.

#5 Laugh together 100 times a day.

#4 Don't think alike; think *together.*

#3 To keep your marriage brimming
With love in the loving cup,
If ever you're wrong, admit it,
If ever you're right, shut up.
—Ogden Nash

#2 Before you give your husband a piece of your mind, make sure *you* can spare it.

#1 Kiss till the cows come home.

—Beamont and Fletcher, *Scornful Lady*

EPILOGUE

Running the Race . . . Together

Your most memorable moments are being formed right now.

● ● ●

A FEW YEARS AGO, something very special happened at the Special Olympics. The smiley-faced competitors were lined up for the 100-yard dash. At the starting signal, all took off, intent on pursuing the goal of the finish line and winning the prize.

As one of the runners rounded a corner, he fell. Tears streamed down the young boy's cheeks as he sat on the tracks, feeling defeated, worthless, and hurt.

What happened next is one of the most memorable moments in sports history. *All* of the Special Olympic runners turned back toward the little boy. They gathered around him, linked arms around him, and *together* they walked to the finish line.

There was not a dry eye in the stadium.

What made this particular moment so memorable? Because it was so counter to our human nature of selfishly going after our own goals. When a woman hurt her leg badly in the regular Olympics, no one turned back to help her. Not one. If they had, do you know what kind of press coverage that would have received? It would've been the event of the year. Sports' Most Unforgettable Moment.

But these Special Olympics runners, although intent on their personal race for the goal, all stopped to put one little boy first. They were a family, joined together in running the race. They had a sensitivity toward each other because each realized he or she had weaknesses too. It could have been any of them who fell that day.

The Special Olympics runners may not have won any individual medals that day, but they did what was most important—they ran the race *together*. And that made them all winners, not only in the eyes of others but in their own hearts, where it really matters.

You and your man are also running a race every day. As both of you pursue your individual goals, will you stop and turn back to help each other along the way? Will you be a family, bonded together for a common goal?

It is only as you run the race together—as man and woman—that you will grow in grace and understanding not only of each other, but of yourself.

You may not win individual prizes, but you'll win the best prize of all: a satisfying marriage for a lifetime.

He will be respected, needed, and fulfilled by you.

You will receive from him daily affection, open, honest communication, and commitment to your family.

You will have the marriage you've always wanted.

QUIZZES & QUIZ ANSWERS

FROM BACK COVER

What your man wants the most:
- A. Sex
- B. Dinner
- C. More of A
- D. Respect
- E. Money and success

Answer: A, C, D in part. But a man's top three needs are to be respected, needed, and fulfilled (and being fulfilled means much more than just sex) *by you.*

How often does a man think about sex?
- A. As much as you
- B. 10 times as much as you
- C. 33 times as much as you
- D. Every day but April 15
- E. Only on days that end in the letter Y

Answer: C

FROM INTRODUCTION

How satisfied are you?
- A. I could be with my man 24 hours a day and still want more. I never want to be away from him.
- B. I love my guy, but it's nice to have a girlfriend break every once in a while.
- C. The male testosterone fest in the garage is about to drive me crazy. Do I, a female, matter at all here?
- D. Anybody here want to switch spouses for a day, a week, a year?

Answers:
- A. You're still on your honeymoon. Just wait until your husband gets the flu.
- B. Good for you. You're thinking straight. Guys need guys as friends, and women need girlfriends. If you both get that kind of time, your marriage will be stronger for it because you won't be tempted to try to turn your tough guy into a girlfriend.

C. Sounds like your boy is being that—a boy. You may need to remind him (gently) of a few of his grown-up responsibilities. If all else fails, wave a pair of your slinkiest panties under his nose when he pokes his head into the kitchen to get a soda. You'll be amazed by how fast those boys will disappear from your garage. And after your own little "fest," your husband will be much more willing to pay attention to you and the tasks you need done around the house.

D. You need to talk with your spouse. Note that I didn't say *confront* your spouse. As soon as you can, and in a warm, inviting environment (free of dogs and children), tell your husband how much you love him. Pour it on. Tell him how much he means to you and how important he is in your life. Tell him how much you respect him and need him. Tell him how important it is to you that he feels fulfilled in your marriage—and that you do too. Then carefully broach the subject that is bothering you, using "I" language. "I could be misreading the situation, but I feel hurt when . . ." Keep away from the "you" accusing finger or tone. Realize that we men are sometimes "dumb as mud" about relationships. We need things spelled out for us, but *always, always* with respect.

FROM #1 THING HE'LL NEVER TELL YOU

How are you communicating?

There are many types of conversations you can exchange with your spouse.

*   Clichés
*   Facts
*   Ideas/opinions
*   Needs/feelings
*   Complete personal truthfulness

Categorize each of the following statements with a *C* for Cliches, an *F* for Facts, an *I* for Ideas/Opinions, an *N* for Needs/Feelings, or a *P* for Personal Truthfulness.

____ "Good morning, honey!"

____ "Could you be home right after work on Wednesday? I need your help to get things thrown together before the Lewises come over for dinner."

____ "I miss Sadie. Could we get another dog?"

____ "I'll be home at five o'clock tonight."

____ "Francine just told me that Jordan joined the military. She and her husband were shocked."

____ "Since I saw that TV program about breast cancer, it's been on my mind. I worry that I might get it sometime. Then what would happen to you? the kids?"

_____ "Do you think we should set aside some money for a special vacation next year since it's our tenth anniversary?"

_____ "And how was your day?"

_____ "It's going to be cold today."

_____ "I'm taking Angie shopping for a new coat. She's growing."

_____ "Ever since mom died, I can't shake this lonely feeling I have. I felt like I've lost not only my mom, but part of myself."

Answers:

C "Good morning, honey!"

N "Could you be home right after work on Wednesday? I really need your help to get things thrown together before the Lewises come over for dinner."

N "I really miss Sadie. Could we get another dog?"

F "I'll be home at five o'clock tonight."

F "Francine just told me that Jordan joined the military. She and her husband were shocked."

P "Since I saw that TV program about breast cancer, it's really been on my mind. I worry that I might get it sometime. Then what would happen to you? the kids?"

I "Do you think we should set aside some money for a special vacation next year since it's our tenth anniversary?"

C "And how was your day?"

F "It's going to be really cold today."

F "I'm taking Angie shopping for a new coat. She's growing."

P "Ever since mom died, I can't shake this lonely feeling I have. I feel like I've lost not only my mom, but part of myself."

Which of the types of conversations are most common in your relationship? Why?

FROM #2 THING HE'LL NEVER TELL YOU

Why won't a man stop for directions?

    A. It's beneath him.

    B. He's got to figure it out himself.

    C. He knows where he's going.

    D. He doesn't like to ask others for help.

    E. Because he doesn't have to go to the john yet.

    F. He thinks, _I can still pull this off._

Answer: None of the above. It's because he worked so hard to pass all those cars.

FROM #3 THING HE'LL NEVER TELL YOU

If he cleans the entire house and offers to take you to Talbot's to buy you a few outfits
- A. he just bought a new set of golf clubs for way too much money.
- B. he cheated on you.
- C. he realized this morning that your anniversary was in February and not in May.
- D. he thinks you need a little sprucing up.
- E. he's hoping to get lucky tonight.

Answer: He finally ordered that boat he always wanted but doesn't have the guts to tell you yet. He figures you'll be much happier about the news after your own shopping spree!

FROM #4 THING HE'LL NEVER TELL YOU

Do you know this woman?

Do you ever find yourself
- A. saying yes when you mean no, no, *No!*?
- B. laughing at a joke you don't understand so no one will feel bad (and you don't look humor deprived)?
- C. vowing never to chair the women's bazaar again? (The problem is you've said that for six years running.)
- D. smiling and complimenting your mother-in-law on her cooking when you absolutely loathe it?
- E. refusing to send your salmon back to a restaurant's kitchen when it arrives on your plate and it's still swimming?

Answer: If you have identified with even *one* of these statements, you are most definitely a pleaser. But if you're aware of this, it doesn't have to control your life.

Do you know this man?
- A. He's always right.
- B. He speaks about women with anger and disrespect.
- C. When he's wrong, it's someone else's fault.
- D. When things don't go his way, he throws an adult temper tantrum or withdraws into icy silence.
- E. After an argument, he equates making love with making up.
- F. He has to win in everything—business, ping-pong, and in love.
- G. He often complains that his employers or supervisors don't know what they're doing.
- H. He's skillful at making you feel guilty, even though you know you were right and you're doing the right thing.

Answer: If you identified your guy as having even one of these traits, you married a controller. But you don't need to let him run all over you.

This quiz is adapted from Dr. Kevin Leman's book, *Pleasers* (Grand Rapids, MI: Fleming H. Revell, 2006).

FROM #5 THING HE'LL NEVER TELL YOU

What do researchers tell us about when men prefer to have sex?
- A. Any day, any time
- B. At the beginning of the day
- C. At the end of the day
- D. All day

Answer: Men don't need a time, just a place.

What do researchers tell us about when women prefer to have sex?
- A. Any day, any time
- B. Early morning, before hair and makeup are done or could be messed up
- C. After a romantic dinner
- D. After the kids are tucked in bed
- E. When the kids aren't home

Answer: None of the above. Women prefer to have sex in the month of June! Seriously, what researchers tell us is that women prefer to have sex in the evening, as opposed to the morning.

FROM #6 THING HE'LL NEVER TELL YOU

Offering your girlfriend's husband your leftover filet mignon at dinner is
- A. not a problem. After all, that steak tasted like roadkill, but Phil will eat anything.
- B. a kind and thoughtful gesture (Phil still looked hungry).
- C. a sure way to cut your fat intake for the day in half.
- D. gross. You offered it because he looked so eager but never dreamed he'd take you up on it.

Answer: None of the above. It's a violation of the unwritten husband code: What is yours is his, and he gets first right of refusal.

FROM #7 THING HE'LL NEVER TELL YOU

Why it's difficult for your man to be your hero
- A. Because you do everything so well—and do it all.

B. You're so busy.

C. You don't stand still long enough for him to help or to please you.

D. Because he's afraid that you'll find fault with whatever he does.

Answer: All of the above, and more!

FROM CONCLUSION: TALKING HIS LANGUAGE

What is your guy's love language?

    A. Words of affirmation

    B. Quality time

    C. Gifts

    D. Acts of service

    E. Physical touch

Answer: Only you can know this, and if you don't, listen to what your guy complains about. That will tell you loudly and clearly!

What is most important to you?

    A. Hearing "I love you, honey" verbally or in a card.

    B. Spending relaxed time with your man—just the two of you.

    C. Getting flowers not for a special occasion but just because he loves you.

    D. When he cleans the bathroom for you and it's not even his turn.

    E. Getting a kiss every time he walks in or out of the door.

Answer: Only you can know this. So why don't you clue in your guy, rather than having him guess?

Introduction: What a Man Really Craves . . .

1. D. Mace and R. Mace, "Enriching Marriages: The Foundation Stone of Family Strength," in *Family Strengths: Positive Models for Family Life,* ed. Nick Stinnett et. al. (Lincoln, Neb.: University of Nebraska Press, 1980), 197-215.
2. Peter Ustinov, "Points to Ponder," *Reader's Digest*, October 1992.

#1 Thing He'll Never Tell You

1. Deborah Tannen, *You Just Don't Understand* (New York: Quill, HarperCollins, 2001), 42.
2. Ibid., 81–82.
3. Ibid., 82–83.
4. Ibid., 297.

#2 Thing He'll Never Tell You

1. For more information on this, see my book, *What a Difference a Daddy Makes* (Nashville, TN: Thomas Nelson Publishers, 2000).
2. For more on this topic, see my book, *Making Your Children Mind without Losing Yours* (Grand Rapids, MI: Fleming H. Revell, 2000).
3. Paul Candon, "Brain Structure May Influence Male-Female Behavior Differences," *Cerebral Cortex,* December 1999.
4. Jane Everhart, "Male, Female Differences Can Impact Treatment Regimens," *New York Times* Syndicate, December 28, 1999.
5. Ibid.
6. Genesis 2:18
7. *The Quest Study Bible,* New International Version, commentary on page 5 for Genesis 2–3.
8. For more on this topic, see my book, *The Birth Order Book* (Grand Rapids, MI: Fleming H. Revell, 1985, 1992).

#3 Thing He'll Never Tell You

1. Matthew 10:8
2. Luke 6:38
3. Proverbs 21:26

#4 Thing He'll Never Tell You

1. For more on this topic, see my book, *Pleasers* (Grand Rapids, MI: Fleming H. Revell, 1987, 2006).

#5 Thing He'll Never Tell You

1. Alan Booth and David Johnson, "Premarital Co-habitation and Marital Success," *Journal of Family Issues* 9 (1988): 261–70. This and several other citations in this section are taken from Wade Horn, *Father Facts* (Gaithersburg, MD: The National Fatherhood Initiative, third edition, no date given), 46ff.
2. Jude 21, TLB
3. Nancy Stedman, "Love Your Body," *Redbook* (May 2001): 46.
4. Susan Crain Bakos, "The Sex Trick Busy Couples Swear By," *Redbook* (2001): 125.
5. Ibid.
6. "You Told Us," *Redbook* (February 2001): 12.
7. My book *Sex Begins in the Kitchen: Because Love Is an All-Day Affair* (Grand Rapids, MI: Fleming H. Revell, 1981, 1992, 1999) addresses this topic and much more.

6 Thing He'll Never Tell You

1. Ephesians 4:15
2. Ephesians 5:33

#7 Thing He'll Never Tell You

1. Lisa Beamer with Ken Abraham, *Let's Roll! Ordinary People, Extraordinary Courage* (Carol Stream, IL: Tyndale House Publishers, 2002), an incredible read by the wife of Todd Beamer. Through it, you will find hope, inspiration, and strength for your own journey.
2. John Eldredge, *Wild at Heart* (Nashville: Thomas Nelson, 2001), 10.
3. Ibid., 15.
4. Ephesians 5:25
5. Dr. Gary Smalley, *The DNA of Relationships* (Carol Stream, IL: Tyndale, 2004), 158, 160.
6. William F. Harley Jr., *His Needs, Her Needs for Parents* (Grand Rapids, MI: Fleming H. Revell, 2003), 112.
7. Joshua 24:15
8. Ecclesiastes 4:12

Conclusion: Talking His Language

1. Some of the material in this conclusion has been adapted from my book, *Sex Begins in the Kitchen: Because Love Is an All-Day Affair* (Grand Rapids, MI: Fleming H. Revell, 1981, 1992, 1999), 167–79.
2. Gary Chapman, *The Five Love Languages* (Chicago: Northfield Publishing, 1995).
3. Ibid., 75.

Epilogue: Running the Race . . . Together

1. Story adapted from "Who Lifts You? And Who Do You Lift?" *The Word for Today* (October 2, 2006): 21.

ABOUT DR. KEVIN LEMAN

Practical Wisdom with a Belly Laugh

● ● ●

AN INTERNATIONALLY KNOWN PSYCHOLOGIST, radio and television personality, and speaker, Dr. Kevin Leman has taught and entertained audiences worldwide with his wit and commonsense psychology.

The best-selling and award-winning author has made house calls for hundreds of radio and television programs, including *The View* with Barbara Walters, *Today, Oprah,* CBS's *The Early Show, Live with Regis Philbin,* CNN's *American Morning,* and *LIFE Today* with James Robison. Dr. Leman has served as a contributing family psychologist to *Good Morning America.*

Dr. Leman is also the founder and president of Couples of Promise, an organization designed and committed to helping couples remain happily married.

Dr. Leman's professional affiliations include the American Psychological Association, American Federation of Television and Radio Artists, National Register of Health Services Providers in Psychology, and the North American Society of Adlerian Psychology.

In 1993, he was the recipient of the Distinguished Alumnus Award of North Park University in Chicago. In 2003, he also received the highest award that a university can extend to their own: the Alumni Achievement Award at the University of Arizona.

Dr. Leman attended North Park University. He received his bachelor's degree in psychology from the University of Arizona, where he later earned his master's and doctorate degrees. Originally from Williamsville, New York, he and his wife, Sande, live in Tucson. They have five children.

For information regarding speaking availability, business consultations, or seminars, please contact:

DR. KEVIN LEMAN
P.O. Box 35370
Tucson, Arizona 85740

Phone: (520) 797-3830
Fax: (520) 797-3809
www.lemanbooksandvideos.com

Resources by Dr. Kevin Leman

Books for Adults

The Birth Order Book

Sheet Music: Uncovering the Secrets of Sexual Intimacy in Marriage

Making Children Mind without Losing Yours

Sex Begins in the Kitchen: Creating Intimacy to Make Your
Marriage Sizzle

7 Things He'll Never Tell You . . . But You Need to Know

What Your Childhood Memories Say about You . . . And What You
Can Do about It

Running the Rapids: Guiding Teenagers through the Turbulent
Waters of Adolescence

What a Difference a Daddy Makes

The Way of the Shepherd *(written with William Pentak)*

Home Court Advantage

Becoming the Parent God Wants You to Be

Becoming a Couple of Promise

A Chicken's Guide to Talking Turkey with Your Kids about Sex
(written with Kathy Flores Bell)

First-Time Mom: Getting Off on the Right Foot (from Birth to
First Grade)

Keeping Your Family Strong in a World Gone Wrong

Step-parenting 101

The Perfect Match

Be Your Own Shrink: 4 Ways to a Better You

Say Good-bye to Stress

Single Parenting That Works: Six Keys to Raising Happy, Healthy
Children in a Single-Parent Home

RESOURCES BY DR. KEVIN LEMAN

When Your Best Isn't Good Enough

Pleasers: Why Women Don't Have to Make Everyone Happy
to Be Happy

Books for Children, with Kevin Leman II

My Firstborn, There's No One Like You

My Middle Child, There's No One Like You

My Youngest, There's No One Like You

My Only Child, There's No One Like You

My Adopted Child, There's No One Like You

My Grandchild, There's No One Like You

DVD/Video Series

Making Children Mind without Losing Yours (Christian—
parenting edition)

Making Children Mind without Losing Yours (Mainstream—public-
school teacher edition)

Value-Packed Parenting: Raising Rock-Solid Kids in a Pleasure-
Driven World

Making the Most of Marriage

Running the Rapids: Guiding Teenagers through the Turbulent Waters of
Adolescence

Single Parenting That Works: Six Keys to Raising Happy, Healthy
Children in a Single-Parent Home

Bringing Peace and Harmony to the Blended Family

Available at 1-800-770-3830 or www.lemanbooksandvideos.com

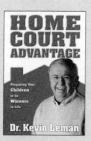